Light from the Hill

ZONDERVAN HEARTH BOOKS

Available from your Christian Bookseller

Book Number

Hearth Romances

2	*The Deepening Stream*	Francena Arnold
3	*Fruit for Tomorrow*	Francena Arnold
4	*Light in My Window*	Francena Arnold
5	*The Barrier*	Sallie Lee Bell
6	*By Strange Paths*	Sallie Lee Bell
7	*The Last Surrender*	Sallie Lee Bell
9	*Romance Along the Bayou*	Sallie Lee Bell
10	*The Scar*	Sallie Lee Bell
11	*The Substitute*	Sallie Lee Bell
12	*Through Golden Meadows*	Sallie Lee Bell
13	*Until the Day Break*	Sallie Lee Bell
16	*This Side of Tomorrow*	Ruth Livingston Hill
17	*Give Me Thy Vineyard*	Guy Howard
19	*Judith*	N. I. Saloff-Astakhoff
20	*Trumpets in the Morning*	Lon Woodrum
21	*Light From the Hill*	Sallie Lee Bell
22	*The Bond Slave*	Sallie Lee Bell
27	*The Queen's Jest*	Sallie Lee Bell
28	*Young Man, Young Man*	Eda Stertz
30	*Til Night Is Gone*	Phyllis Primmer

Hearth Classics

29	*Right On With Love*	Lon Woodrum
31	*The Warm Summer*	Craig Massey

Hearth Mysteries

8	*The Long Search*	Sallie Lee Bell
14	*Candle of the Wicked*	Elizabeth Brown

Sebastian Thrillers

23	*Code Name Sebastian*	James L. Johnson
24	*The Nine Lives of Alphonse*	James L. Johnson
25	*A Handful of Dominoes*	James L. Johnson
26	*A Piece of the Moon is Missing*	James L. Johnson

HEARTH
BOOKS

A HEARTH ROMANCE

Light from the Hill

Sallie Lee Bell

ZONDERVAN
PUBLISHING HOUSE

OF THE ZONDERVAN CORPORATION | GRAND RAPIDS, MICHIGAN 49506

REFERENCES

Judaism — Creed and Life, Morris Joseph
Holidays and Festivals, Ben Edidin

LIGHT FROM THE HILL
Copyright 1965 by Zondervan Publishing House
Grand Rapids, Michigan

Library of Congress Catalog Card No. 65-19511

ISBN 0-310-21082-8

First Hearth Books Edition 1978
Fifth printing 1981

Printed in the United States of America

1

Faith Marshall lounged in a chair, watching her mother busily knitting. Her mother, Martha, seemed to always be busy. If she was not in the kitchen stirring up a delicious cake or preparing one of her favorite dishes, she was working among her flowers. Or if there was nothing else to engage her time, she was certain to be involved in what Faith called her "eternal knitting."

Her mother knitted so rapidly that the needles fairly flew in and out of the stitches she was piling up from one needle to another.

Suddenly her mother paused for a moment and looked at her lovely daughter. She smiled as the needles rested for a moment.

"Why so pensive?" she asked.

"I was wondering what you would do if you had nothing to do and could sit like I'm sitting, resting and enjoying leisure. It's wonderful if you could only relax for a little while and see how it feels."

"I don't seem to be able to do that," her mother replied. Her eyes looked off into space as if she were seeing something that Faith couldn't see. "I suppose it's because I was taught never to waste time. My mother always impressed upon me from the earliest I can remember, that life was given to us to make the most of it and that time was not to be wasted because, after all, there was so little of it in this life of ours, no matter how long we lived.''

"Yet you say that Grandmother was kind and gentle. That sounds as if she were a slave driver,'' Faith remarked thoughtlessly.

"She was the dearest mother a girl ever had,'' her mother replied with a note of rebuke in her voice. "I'm sorry she never lived long enough for you to know her.''

"I'm sorry I said that, Mother,'' Faith apologized. She leaned over and kissed her mother upon her cheek. "You're mistaken, though. You are the best mother a girl ever had. And you make me ashamed of myself for wasting time like this when I could be doing something useful instead of lolling around. What can I do to help you?''

"Nothing, dear,'' her mother replied with a tender smile. "Times have changed and you're just a little different from me and the way I was brought up. My mother still had her traditions and she could never get away from them. I still remember them and though I have tried to change for your father's sake, I can't forget many of them. That's why I like to keep busy.''

"Tell me something, Mother,'' Faith said after a moment's silence. "You never have told me and I never thought to ask until now. Funny I never thought of asking before. But then maybe you wouldn't have told me before, for perhaps I was too young to understand. How did Grandmother feel when you fell in love with Dad? Was she bitter and did she make it hard for you when you told her that you wanted to marry Dad?''

Her mother was silent for a while and a look of sadness shadowed to her dark, expressive eyes.

"I hated to hurt her, but I loved your father so much that I could never give him up, no matter how much it might hurt her for me to marry him. She was hurt and she begged me not to marry out of my faith and my people. She was afraid that it would bring God's wrath down upon all of us, for she still believed the law of Moses that a child of Jacob should not marry a Gentile.

"When I told her what it would mean to me, if I had to give Harry up, she said she wouldn't put a stumbling block in my way. I think, though, that it broke her heart and perhaps shortened her life. That's the burden of grief that I'll carry with me until the end."

"I'm sorry, Mother," Faith murmured. Then, after a pause, "Why did she make you promise to name me Faith?"

"She hoped that you would grow up to be a true child of Israel, that you would not follow your Gentile father in his belief in a false Messiah," her mother said slowly. "I promised, though I knew that I could never carry out her wish about training you in the beliefs of her people and mine. I loved your father so much that I wanted to be everything that he was and that he wanted for you, for he adored you from the moment you uttered your first feeble wail." A tender smile flitted across her lips, driving away the shadow.

"He's the dearest Dad in the whole world," Faith remarked with a warm note in her voice. "Is that why you never attend your synagogue?" she asked.

"Yes, that's why, though it grieves me that I can't worship the God of my ancestors nor observe the holy days as I used to do. That's the price I pay for my love, but I'm willing to pay it, even though I die without hope."

"Why should you die without hope?" Faith asked with concern.

"It is the word of the Law," her mother told her.

"But Dad doesn't go to his church very often," Faith argued, "and here I am, left alone in the middle without any faith at all. What a joke my name is!" .

"Let's hope that it will all come out right some day," her mother replied as she put up her knitting and went into the kitchen.

Faith sat thinking of what her mother had said. She saw the knitting lying where her mother had left it. She knew that her mother would pick it up in the evening while her father read the paper and then nodded while they watched television. The garment her mother was knitting would soon be a lovely sweater which would be the envy of all Faith's friends when she wore it.

It was true, what she had said. Between her mother's Jewish faith and her father's nominal faith in his religion, she was left with nothing tangible spiritually. She remembered that she had been taken to Sunday school by her father when she was quite young and she had enjoyed the stories of David and Samson and her mother had been happy when she had repeated what she had heard, but when she grew older and began to learn New Testament stories concerning Jesus and His ministry and to ask questions about Him, she rebelled in her heart, for she feared that Faith would be turned away from the belief in the one true God and the Messiah who was still to come. She told her husband how she felt and he did not insist upon taking Faith any longer. She hoped that she could teach Faith what she remembered about her own faith and the hope in the Messiah who was yet to come.

Presently Faith rose and went to her room to change her dress. Keith would soon be coming for her in his new car and she was eager to have her first ride in it.

She could hear her mother singing as she went toward the kitchen to tell her that she would soon be leaving. Her heart stirred with pity for her mother and her problem. She had not known until now what a weight her mother had carried all these years, even though she was so happy with her husband.

She stood for a moment in the doorway and admired her mother's profile as she bent over her work. Her mother had the dark eyes and black curly hair that was characteristic of her race, but her features were not truly Jewish. The short straight nose which Faith had inherited, gave her a patrician beauty, a beauty that had won the yeart of young Harry Marshall. Faith was much like her mother, though her hair was dark brown instead of black. Her delicately curved lips parted in a tender smile as she called to her mother and told her good-by.

"I'll be back early, Mother," she said.

She heard the sound of the car through the open window as she hastened to the front door. Her heart was singing happily as she opened the door and greeted the handsome young man approaching. His hair almost matched her own in color, but his eyes were blue.

He smiled, revealing white teeth. "On time, as usual," he remarked as he led her to the car. "I know I'll never be late for work because my wife overslept and didn't get me off in time."

"Who will that wife be, I wonder?" she teased with a roguish smile.

"If she isn't you, then I'll never have one," he asserted as he helped her in and sat beside her.

As they drove away he gave her a fleeting glance, but he kept his attention on the road.

"How many times do I have to ask you before you say yes?" he asked.

"I thought we had settled that question a long time ago," she retorted. "How many years was it? Let me see, I was five and you were seven, or was it six?"

"Six going on seven," he corrected with a little laugh. "My! I thought that when I got to be seven, I'd be almost a man."

"I knew that I wasn't going to let any other girl have you, remember?"

"Yeah," he replied ungrammatically. "Boy! you took possession of me almost from the first day." He gave her a fleeting, tender smile. "Remember?"

"Of course I remember. Haven't you held that up to me every chance you had since the day I said I was going to marry you?"

"I have to, every now and then, when you take off with some other fellow and when he tries to take possession of you, as if you weren't already engaged to me."

"But I'm not," she maintained. "You can't hold the words of a silly little kid against me and I won't have it. I want to have fun with a lot of other fellows before I

11

settle down to marrying someone I really love."

"And who could that be but me?" he asked. "Didn't you tell me that you liked me a lot and that I had to marry you, or else?"

"Yes," and again the roguish smile flitted across her lips, "and I still like you a lot, but that doesn't mean that I intend to marry you. A girl's tastes change as she grows older. Perhaps my taste will change as I grow older. That's why I want to be free to change my mind if I want to."

They had come to the lake and he stopped his car in one of the parking places off the shore road. He turned to her and there was a serious light in his eyes.

"Faith, my dearest, I'm not joking now. I meant every word I said. If I can't have you, I'll never want anyone. I've loved you ever since that day you kissed me against my efforts to stop you, ever since you said you liked me a lot. I loved you then, but I didn't really know what love was. I only knew that I looked for you the first thing when I woke up and the thought of you was with me every waking moment. I cried my eyes out, almost, when my parents moved across town and I couldn't play with you any more except on rare occasions. You haven't forgotten, have you?"

"I don't want to remember embarrassing moments," she replied.

"Please be serious," he begged. "I may have to go into service soon and I can't go without your promise to marry me. I love you so much, Faith. Do you love me or is it only friendship? You've put me off so long. I can't wait any longer. Which is it?"

She suddenly lost her teasing mood and fear took its place. The thought that he would soon have to leave when he entered the service filled her with dismay. He had filled her whole life since that day they had played together and she had announced her determination to marry him.

The years that he would be away would seem like an eternity.

She turned to him and her eyes were filled with a new

light while her face flushed and her breath came in a little joyful gasp.

"It's love, Keith. You should know that. I've only been playing around with these other boys because I wanted to have a little fun. But it's been you all along. I don't have to tell you. I love you and I never want to belong to anyone else but you."

He took her in his arms and their lips met in the first kiss she had ever allowed since they were little children and she had forced him to let her kiss him as she overcame his boyish dislike of kisses.

"You've made me the happiest man in the world," he murmured as he held her. "Sometimes I hoped and often I doubted, for you were so unpredictable. Now that I know, those two years in the service will seem like nothing. I can come home on furlough and I'll be looking forward to that, every day that I'm away from you."

Later, as they drove home he remarked, "We forgot all about my new car. How do you like it?"

"It's beautiful," she told him. "It's a pity that you'll have to leave it so soon."

"They won't call me until I finish the course I'm taking. They said it would be important to defense purposes later on and I'll get an extension of my time until I finish. I'll have some months left yet until I finish and take my examination in this course. The car will keep until I get back."

"You played a trick on me!" she cried. "You talked as if you would be going right away. You should be ashamed of yourself!"

"All's fair in love and war," he quoted. "I didn't see why I had to give the exact number of days before I'll be leaving."

Breaking the rules of safe driving, he put an arm around her and drew her to him as they drove toward her home.

2

"I wonder what your mother will say when you tell her about us," Keith asked as he helped her out of the car.

"I don't want to tell her just yet," she told him. "Let us have these few months together before you leave, free from any worry about what our parents might think if they know that we're engaged."

"I wonder if that will be best," he remarked soberly. "They'll have to know sometime, so why not now?"

"Because," she explained illogically. "I know they suspect that we're in love and I know how my mother might feel if she knew the truth. I don't want her to be hurt until she has to know. In the meantime I can be free from that worry. It'll be time enough for her to know when you get out of the service. I'm sure your mother hopes that you'll marry some-one else — not a girl like me who's half Jewish."

"I know she wishes I'd marry a girl who is a real Christian, for she is one," he said rather sadly. "I know she wishes above everything that I'll become a Christian. That's her constant prayer. She told me that many times."

"Then I know she'd hate to see you marry me," and Faith's voice held a note of sadness. "Have I kept you from becoming the kind of Christian she wants you to be?''

"No, I don't think you have," he answered thoughtfully. "Somehow I've never felt the desire to become the kind of a believer that she is. I believe in God and I believe that Jesus Christ is His Son, but that's as far as I've ever gone and I just don't feel the desire to go any further."

"But you know that I don't believe in your Christ at all," she argued. "I believe like Mother does, that one day the Messiah will come, but it won't be Jesus of Nazareth. I know that if we do get married, that will always be a barrier between us."

"I promise you that it won't be," he declared. "It is no barrier between your mother and father, so why worry about any barrier between us?"

She smiled faintly. "Dad is so good and he loves my mother so much that nothing could ever come between them. I know that he might wish that she would go to church with him, but then, he seldom goes himself and they never talk about religion. That is taboo in my home."

"I'll do as you say about not telling them," he said. "We won't tell them until I return and we can make plans. And the subject of religion need never come up in our home. I'll be just as devoted as your dad could ever be, for I love you so much, Faith, darling. You've been the center of my life ever since I can remember and life wouldn't be worth living without hope of having you."

Faith was singing a happy little song as he left her and she went inside. She had loved Keith as much and as long as he had said he loved her, but until today she had never been sure that he wanted to marry her, though he had told her so many times.

She remembered that day when she had planted a wet kiss upon his cheek. She had aimed that kiss at his lips, but he had, with the dislike of a little boy to being kissed, turned his lips away. She remembered that she had insisted that she was going to marry him and he had objected vigorously to the idea. He didn't want to marry any girl, for he disliked all little girls except her, but as time passed, she so impressed him with her determination to marry him that he had accepted the idea and had finally agreed that it was a good one. Now he had seriously accepted that little girl idea and really wanted her for his wife.

She hated knowing she would eventually have to tell her mother, for she knew that she would be hurt and disappointed. She had known something of her mother's life, of her grandfather coming to America as an immigrant and how he had made a fortune in just a few years. He had the ability to make money, an ability which God had given to his nationality, and he had been generous and indulgent with his family.

He loved his daughter Martha with a passionate love that was almost idolatry. Though he had wanted a son, when he knew that his wife could never have another child, he accepted the knowledge and forgot his disappointment, for he loved his wife with all the power of his being. He had great plans for Martha and she was reared in strictest observance of their faith.

When Martha met Harry Marshall and began to go with him, her father forbade her to continue their friendship, for he didn't want her to associate with any boy who was not a Jew.

Martha hated to disobey her father, but she had fallen in love with Harry. She finally confessed to her mother that she wanted to marry him. As she had told Faith, it broke her mother's heart, but she knew that there was nothing she could do, for the worst had happened and she remembered her own youth and that she had loved her husband enough to have given up everything for him, if that had been necessary.

When Martha's father knew the truth, he was furious and he told Martha that if she did not give Harry up and marry some Jewish boy, she would no longer be a daughter of his.

To please her mother, Martha was married in both the Protestant ceremony and in the Jewish marriage ritual. Her father refused to attend either ceremony and he disowned her. Not long afterward he died of a heart attack and Martha felt that she had been the cause of it.

Though her heart was broken and she herself was broken in health, Martha's mother still loved her child and clung to her in spite of disappointment and sorrow. She lived alone, though Martha and her husband begged her to live with them. When Martha knew that she was going to have a child, she succeeded in persuading her mother to live with her until after the baby came. She promised her mother that she would name the baby Faith if it should be a girl. Her mother told her that this would be a reminder to rear the child in the religion of her ancestors.

Her mother, as she had told Faith, never lived to see the baby, for she died before the baby was born. Martha felt that she had hastened her mother's death. She had always been frail and the shock of her husband's death had been more than she could bear.

Faith didn't want the same thing to happen to her mother. That was one reason why she didn't want to tell her until she had to. Another reason, which she didn't tell Keith, was that she didn't want anyone else to know of their engagement. She wanted to continue going with other boys. When Keith left, she would be lonesome and if other boys knew that she was engaged, they would leave her alone. She wanted to have all the fun possible before she settled down to married life.

When she came inside, her father was already there. He was reading the paper while her mother was putting the finishing touches to the evening meal. He looked up when she entered and gave her a smile.

"How's my girl today?" he asked as she came and sat beside him.

He put an arm around her and drew her to him.

"Just about as happy as a girl could be," she said unguardedly.

He gave her a quizzical look and smiled indulgently. "All because that young rascal took you off to parts unknown in that shiny new car?"

"Oh, that's just a little part of the whole joy of life," she evaded, trying to cover up her slip. "I'm just happy to be alive and well and able to enjoy every minute that I'm living."

"Keep up that spirit, little one, as long as you can," he advised. Then he put the paper down and they both went into the dining room at the call to dinner.

Though Mrs. Marshall had a maid, which they could well afford, still she liked to superintend the cooking and she wanted Faith to learn about cooking and housekeeping. There might come a day when there would not be so much money and she would need to know how to manage. She had been taught the same provision by her own mother, for, deeply rooted within her mother's memory was the heritage from the days when her people did not have even the bare necessities and they had learned to make a little go a long way.

"How did you enjoy your ride?" her mother asked when they had sat down to the meal.

"Had a grand time," Faith told her. "That new car is a gem and Keith is mighty proud of it. He's going into the service right after graduation. I'd forgotten about that. I'll be missing him."

This was good news to her mother. She hoped that before Keith returned, Faith would have lost her interest in him. She liked Keith, but he was not Jewish and her one hope was that Faith would not do as she had done, but that she would fall in love with some Jewish boy who would make her happy and at the same time make herself feel that she had fulfilled at least a part of her mother's hopes for the grandchild she never knew.

"You and Keith have been pals for a long time," her father remarked. "When you were kids, I thought that you would drag him to the altar in spite of his objections," and he chuckled at the memory.

"I thought I would have to drag him," and Faith joined in his laughter, "but when I grew older, I realized that it was the man's place to lead the girl, even if she did drag him there without him being aware of it."

"Is that what you're still trying to do?" her father asked with a twinkle in his eye.

"I don't want a husband that I'd have to drag anywhere," she replied. "I'm glad we're still friends, but I don't want to settle down to marriage for a while yet. I want all the fun I can get before I get married and have a little pest like I was, to make life miserable for me."

Her mother gave her a tender smile.

"You never were that, honey. You were always a joy, even when I had to spank you."

Faith and her father both laughed as Faith said, "And I know there was real joy in that, Mother, for I sure deserved it and got a lot of it."

That night when her mother and father were alone preparing for bed, he remarked, "I know what you're thinking. You're hoping that when that boy leaves for the service, Faith will lose interest in him. I hope for your sake that she will. I don't want to see you hurt, dear," and he took her in his arms and held her close.

She let the tears fall, for she was thinking of her mother and how she had hurt her.

"Let's not talk about it," she said brokenly. "We promised never to talk about this. I hope for the best for Faith. I'll try to take whatever comes to her if it will make her happy."

"I'll say amen to that," he said tenderly. "I hope she will be as happy as we have been, as happy as I have tried to make you."

"As happy as you have made me," she replied tremulously.

She fell asleep with a heavy heart, however, for she was thinking of what her happiness had done to her own mother and she wondered if there was forgiveness for a thing like that and if there was, from where it would come.

3

Now that she was sure that at last she belonged to Keith, Faith was so happy that her mother could not help but notice the change in her. She had always had a happy disposition and she didn't let disappointments or little annoyances keep her spirits down for long, but now she was radiant. Finally Mrs. Marshall remarked about it.

"I never saw you look so happy, my dear. What has happened? Something wonderful? I hope so."

She wondered if it had anything to do with Keith. She was hoping that nothing definite would happen between them before Keith had to leave. In two years she would have ample opportunity to become interested in someone else. She liked Keith and could have wished for nothing better for Faith than that they should marry, if Keith had been Jewish. She determined to keep hoping that Faith would meet some Jewish boy whom she could love. She knew that her husband would not care what the boy's faith might be, for he had so little of his own and it meant so much to her.

Faith smiled in answer to her Mother's question. "I'm just happy to be alive. Perhaps it's showing more today than it did before. It's wonderful to be young and able to get the most out of life."

"Are you sure that it has nothing to do with Keith?" her mother persisted and was immediately sorry she had asked.

She didn't want to bring up the subject of Keith, but now she had done it and there was nothing she could say to undo the words.

"If it had to do with Keith, I should be feeling sad instead of so happy, knowing that he'll be leaving soon. I'll miss him, of course," Faith added, feeling guilty because she knew that she wasn't telling the truth. "But there will be others who can help me to forget that I'll be missing him."

"I'm glad you feel that way," her mother remarked with a sigh of relief. "Please don't get involved with Keith before he goes away. I know that you have always been the closest of friends and that you like him a lot, but please let it stay that way until he comes back. I'm sure that he cares for you," her mother continued desperately, now that she had begun the subject that she had determined not to mention, "but let it remain that way at least until he comes back. If he wants you to be tied to him with a promise, you'll be more lonesome than ever and you'll be unhappy because you won't have any attention from other boys. Wait until he comes back before you make any promise to him, even if you care for him."

"I promise to wait, Mom," Faith assured her. "I don't want to have to sit at home with nothing to do but wish he was here. But tell me this, Mom. If he should come back and should want me to marry him and if I should want to marry him, would you be willing for us to marry or would you be very much hurt?"

"I believe it would break my heart, but I wouldn't oppose you." There was a mist of tears in her eyes.

"Don't grieve too soon, Mother," Faith said, putting an arm around her and kissing her cheek lightly. "Just remember, though," she added playfully, "that I told Keith long ago that I was going to marry him whether or no, so he might just remind me of that determination of mine."

"I remember and I won't worry if you keep your promise," and her mother smiled faintly.

"I shall," Faith maintained, but she knew that she was not telling the truth, for she was already committed to the thing that she had wanted for so long.

Mrs. Marshall was satisfied for the time being, for she knew that Faith would keep her promise. For that reason, she didn't worry when Keith and Faith were together so frequently. She knew that the time was short and she had her own plan to try to make Faith forget him and become interested in someone else.

She forgot for the moment her own love for the boy who had won her heart, and that she had never wavered from that love even though there were many others who would have won her if they could have.

"I feel so guilty," Faith acknowledged to Keith.

Keith didn't have much time to be with her as graduation and his examinations approached. He had a heavy course and wanted to pass with honors.

"My mother thinks we're just friends and I've promised that there would be nothing between us until you come back. I hated to lie to her, but there was no other way. I couldn't bear to make her unhappy, for I'll be so unhappy myself with you away for so long."

"I know how she feels about me and I wonder if she'll ever agree to my marrying you," he said.

"She admitted that it would break her heart, but that she wouldn't make any objections. I asked her how she would feel if we were ever to get married and that's what she said. I wonder how your mother would feel — if she would feel the same way."

"No, my mother is a real Christian, as I've already told you," he told her. "She has told me from her Bible that today there are only two classes of people in the world, saved and lost, and that during this age, the Jews are in the same class with anyone else. She's told me so much about the Bible that I sometimes wonder why I can't do what she is so anxious for me to do, to accept Jesus Christ as my Saviour." He looked at her and smiled rather ruefully. "From what she believes, we're both in the same group. We're both lost."

"Doesn't that frighten you, if it's true?" Faith asked. "It frightens me, just to hear you say that, even if it isn't true."

"It should when I remember what my mother has told me her Bible says, that each one of us must give an account of himself to God. I do feel a little uneasy sometimes, but I never do anything about it. Mother never urges me any more. She used to, but it made me cross, so she said that she wouldn't mention it any more. She would just pray that before it was too late, the Holy Spirit would speak to me and lead me to the Saviour."

"Then you wouldn't be in the same group with me," Faith remarked. "I'd be on the outside and you would be with her in her group, if what she believes is true. Maybe she'd try to win me, but I know she never could. Then she would really be sorry that you had married me."

He laughed. "You're looking a long way ahead, darling. Let's not worry about the future until we come to it. Perhaps by the time we're married and settled down and you get to know her better, you'll be willing to believe as she does. You may even persuade me to be a believer like you."

"That will never be," she declared vehemently. "I can never accept Jesus of Nazareth as the Messiah. Our Messiah is still to come."

"Let's forget it all and talk about something more pleasant. Will you go to the dance with me Saturday at the fraternity house?"

"I wonder," she replied with a happy lilt in her voice and a smile upon her lips. "I might consider it."

He bent over and kissed her swiftly, keeping his eyes on the road ahead.

"That sounds better," he said. "Plenty of time to think of other things when we grow too old to enjoy life as we enjoy it now."

Faith was radiant and lovely in her formal of pale green and her mother's eyes glowed with pride as she observed the girl's beauty. How she wished that the girl's grandmother could have seen her! Martha herself had been quite pretty

23

when she was younger, but she had never been as beautiful as Faith was, with her dark eyes, flawless complexion, and features that blended perfectly.

Keith realized at the dance what a problem he would have when he had to leave Faith, for as soon as she entered, other boys approached and asked for a dance. She was swamped with admirers and Keith could barely save a few dances for himself. He was more jealous than he had ever been before, for until now, Faith had seemed to belong to him completely. She had put others off with one excuse after another when they asked for a date, so that she could be with him, but now she seemed eager to accept the attentions of as many as possible. He was so hurt that he spoke to her about it on their way home.

"You didn't seem to care whether you danced with me at all," he grumbled. "You could have turned a lot of those fellows down, but you didn't."

"Why should I?" she asked defensively. "That was when I didn't know for sure that you cared and before I knew you were going away so soon."

"So, now that you're sure of me, you want to play around with every fellow who shows an interest in you," he accused.

"That's not it," she retorted in hurt tones. "Before, I wanted you to feel that I cared more for you, but now that you know I do and because you'll soon be leaving me, I do want to have some friends to keep me from being lonely and on the shelf while you're away."

"And to help make you forget that you love me. That's not a happy thought," he remarked.

"No one could ever do that, Keith," she said as she snuggled against him. "I've loved you too long and your love has been too much a part of me, for me to ever stop loving you. But I don't want to be lonely while you're gone. Don't be angry with me. No one could make me forget you."

He was somewhat mollified, but he was not happy at the prospect and he was still hurt when he told her good-night and left her.

24

4

The days sped by on swift wings, too swiftly for Faith, for she faced the future which was approaching so rapidly, the time when Keith would be leaving. They were together as often as Keith could manage, for he was trying to finish his regular course and also prepare for an examination for the extra work which he had been taking. If he passed this examination, it would lead to some important work in the government when he was out of the service.

He dreaded the thought of leaving Faith to the attentions of others who were too eager to make an impression upon her, for his peace of mind.

As the season advanced, there were more parties at the college and in the homes of Faith's friends. She went to all of them, for she loved the gay life that they afforded. Her mother did not worry any longer about her, for the time being, for she believed Faith's promise and since Keith would be leaving soon, she would hope that before he returned, some other boy would attract Faith's interest, a boy who was of her own people.

Harry Marshall knew that his wife was concerned about Keith and Faith, and he hoped for her sake, that Faith would marry someone of whom his wife approved. Since his own marriage had been happy in spite of the difference in their beliefs, he didn't care what the boy might believe, just so he was worth-while and could make Faith happy.

There was a young boy, Mark Ledbetter, whom Faith had met at one of the parties she had attended and who had been interested in her from the beginning of their acquaintance. Before she had promised to marry Keith she had not given Mark much encouragement, but now that she was secure in Keith's love and because she knew that he would soon be away, she showed more interest in Mark. Keith noticed this, but he knew that it would do no good to remonstrate with her, for he knew that she would have the same excuse that she had given him before, that she would be lonely and need some fun, and she would assure him that no one could ever take his place. He tried to believe this, but the fact still stirred within him that Faith could be happy in someone else's company, for he didn't even want to look at another girl, much less pay her any attention.

He had argued this with her on one occasion when she had danced with Mark during one of their parties in the gym at college, but she had silenced him with her very effective argument.

"It's different between a man and a woman," she informed him. "If you show a girl marked attention, it's a sure sign that you're interested in her, but with me, it's entirely different, just as I've tried to make you see. Even if some boy is interested in me, that's no sure sign that I'm interested in him, or that I could care for him. I've told you that you have all of my heart and you always will, but I'm glad if some boy likes me well enough to want to date me, because it will help me not to be lonely without you."

"A pretty good argument from your point of view," he argued glumly, "but how about the poor guy you're leading on? Don't you have any pity for him? He'll think you're falling for him and when he knows the truth he'll get a big let-down. How do you think he'll feel? Are you being fair to him?"

She shrugged off the question. "Men are different, as I've said before. Perhaps he may feel let down and I know he'll despise me, but I can't help that. After a while he'll look around for some other girl who'll be more faithful. I haven't seen any boys yet dying of a broken heart. As soon as one affair is smashed, they go out looking for another. If I should fall in love with someone else, you wouldn't die of a broken heart. You'd find someone else and before long you'd wonder how you ever could have loved me."

"I sometimes wonder why I do care so much," he admitted morosely.

She turned a surprised look upon him and in her expressive dark eyes there was deep hurt.

"If you're sorry you do care, there is still time for you to change your mind, Keith." Her lip trembled and she was on the verge of tears.

He looked at her solemnly. "I don't want to change my mind and you know it. Sometimes I've thought that you enjoyed keeping me guessing, just to see me suffer, but even then, I couldn't stop loving you, though I confess I tried. You know that you have me caught — hook, line, and sinker — and you know that I'll never be able to get away, even if I wanted to." A slow smile spread across his lips, driving away the gloom. "And you know that I'll never want to."

She laid her head upon his breast while his arm held her close.

"I'd die if you should ever stop loving me," she murmured. "Please believe that I don't want to flirt or to lead anyone on, but I do want to have a little fun even while I'll be missing you so much. I promise that I'll be careful not to give anyone too much encouragement. Please let's not quarrel about what I'll be doing while you're away. I'll promise not to do anything that would hurt you or anyone else."

He couldn't be too sure about her keeping her promise, for he remembered her promise to her mother, but he had to be content and not to worry. As time passed, however, and she accepted dates with Mark more frequently, he was not only worried, but angry with her. She could at least have waited until he was gone, he thought, before she accepted so much attention from Mark. He knew that she only went with Mark when he couldn't be with her, but that fact didn't make him any less unhappy, nor did it lessen his jealousy.

Mark Ledbetter was good-looking, a brilliant student, and he seemed to have every quality that made a boy interesting to a girl.

When Faith's mother met Mark not long after they had been going together, she was happy to know that he was Faith's friend. She knew that the young man was Jewish. She could see it in his handsome features, the broad cheek bones, the high arch of his nose, the thick curly black hair, and the dark brows over his black eyes.

She told Mark that she had met his mother, for she remembered having met her recently, but the name had escaped her, and later she invited him to have dinner with them.

Mark accepted the invitation eagerly and came not long afterward. It was the first time he had eaten a meal in a home where the Christian blessing was offered, though it was offered rather perfunctorily by Faith's father. Though it was a new experience for him, he wasn't surprised, for he knew that Faith's family was not wholly Jewish and that the head of the house usually led in whatever worship there was.

After this there were other occasions when he was invited to dinner or invited in for a cold drink or some other refreshment when they had been together to some party or a football game.

Keith was not often invited, for there were fewer times when he could have accepted the invitation. There were fewer times when he could be with Faith as the time approached for those important examinations.

Faith was unhappy because she saw so little of Keith and there was so little time left for them to be together. She didn't realize how Keith hated to be deprived of these last few weeks with her and how he seethed with jealousy because he knew that she was with Mark, for she didn't try to conceal the truth from him.

Mrs. Marshall was wise enough to say little about Mark, except a word dropped now and then about how good-looking he was and what a brilliant mind he had. The words were used cautiously and sparingly and, she hoped, at just the right time, so that Faith might not suspect her intentions. But her husband knew and he was just a little worried over the situation. He wondered how it would end and how it might affect Faith's happiness.

He liked the young man and it didn't matter which one of them she might choose, or if it might even be someone else. But he didn't want his wife to influence Faith to do something that might bring grief to her in the end.

"I don't think you should try to encourage that boy or try to influence Faith to become interested in him," he told his wife. "You might do something that you'll regret when it's too late."

"I'd never regret it if she fell in love with Mark," his wife retorted. "He's a fine young fellow, as fine as Keith, and he's Jewish. Nothing would make me happier than for Faith to marry him."

"Are you trying to atone for what you did when you married me?" he asked in hurt tones. "Are you sorry you did what you did? Remember, I never asked you to give up your faith for me. I left that with you."

"I'm not sorry that I married you, my husband, but I am sorry that I had to hurt my parents by doing that. I didn't give up my faith, for I still believe in the one true God and that Messiah will come one day and deliver my people, but I gave up my people and for that perhaps I shall be punished. I don't want Faith to have this same burden of guilt."

"But remember that our daughter has Gentile blood in her as well as Jewish blood and that she has no such obligation as you seem to think you had. You know I never believed that and I've tried to make you believe that I'm right, but I see that I've never succeeded in changing your mind."

"No. I suppose I'm just hardheaded," and she sighed. "But I shall still hope that she'll fall in love with Mark and I'll be glad when Keith is gone."

"Poor Keith! Don't you have any pity for him? I know he's been in love with Faith ever since they were children. I've seen it in his eyes every time he looked at her."

"He's a man and even if he's hurt for a little while, he'll find someone else," she retorted, using Faith's same argument.

"Do you think that's what I would have done, if you should have turned me down?" he asked playfully.

"I never did give you a chance to find out," she answered and kissed him lightly.

5

As the time drew nearer for Keith to take his final examination and he was able to see little of Faith, both of them were unhappy over the situation. He wanted to be with her every moment possible, but he was forced to give most of his time to that important examination, for his whole future might depend upon it.

Faith was not only unhappy, but she was vaguely disturbed over the situation. She knew her mother was pleased over the attention that Mark was paying her and she felt that she would be glad when Keith was out of the picture.

She liked Mark and she enjoyed being with him. He was an entertaining conversationalist. His conversation was not limited to small talk about local affairs and college gossip as were most of the other boys of her acquaintance. His knowledge of world conditions and other affairs, of which she knew little, both interested and enlightened her.

She knew that there were many girls who would have been glad to have Mark for a steady date, for he was not only good-looking, but he was wealthy in his own right through an inheritance from his grandfather. He drove an expensive car and often took her to places that were exclusive and where there was dancing afterward.

Faith felt that she was not only deceiving her mother, but that she was not being fair to Keith, for she knew that he was unhappy over the situation. She was not thinking of Mark at all, except that he met her need.

One evening a climax came when she had been invited to a party at one of the clubs when Keith had been invited, but couldn't attend. Just a few hours before time for the party, he found that he could finish the experiment he had been working on sooner than he had expected and he phoned Faith and told her that he could take her. She told him that she already had a date.

"Can't you break it?" he asked, disappointed.

He had so few evenings left that he felt desperate enough to ask it of her.

"You know I can't do that, Keith," she told him. "You know I'd rather go with you, but if I did this, I'd be on the black list and no one would ask me for another date. You ought to know that."

"I suppose it's with Mark. He seems to be your steady now," he remarked bitterly.

"That's not a very nice remark," she replied in hurt tones. "You can't expect me to sit at home and miss everything, just because you can't take me places on account of that old exam. I don't think that's so important that you couldn't spend a little more time with me, seeing you'll be leaving so soon."

"It's important to both of us, Faith. If I finish this course and pass that examination, I'll be in line for something good when I come home — and that will mean a good living for us. That is, if you still want to marry me when I get out of service."

"You know I do, Keith. What makes you say things like that? You know that I'm only going with Mark and others because I can't have you."

"Then I suppose you won't mind if I find some good-looking girl when I get to the base and give her the rush like Mark's giving you."

"You won't have to go out with some other girl unless you want to," she told him. "You know, like I've said, it's different with you."

"That old argument doesn't hold good," he retorted. "It isn't different with you. You don't have to go with anyone if you don't want to. I'll be just like you say you'll be, when I get on the base. I'll be even more lonesome than you'll be, so why shouldn't I have a little fun if I find someone who's willing to share it with me?"

"You'll do just as you please," she said icily. "I'm sorry I can't go with you tonight, but I can't."

"Can't you explain the situation to Mark?" he persisted. "Tell him that I'll be going away soon and this may be the only time I'll have to go to a party with you."

"And let him know that I'm engaged to you?" she cried. "Of course I can't do that. I couldn't give him any other reason for breaking this date, except to let him know that I'd rather be with you. He'd never ask for another date if I did that. If you come to the party, I promise to save some dances for you if you want me to," she conceded.

"Thanks, but you're too generous," and he hung up.

She was almost in tears and she wasn't happy over the prospect of the party. When Mark came for her, she tried to be as gay and full of life as ever, but she found it hard. She kept thinking of Keith and how hurt he was. She wished that she had broken the date with Mark, for she wanted more than anything to be held in Keith's arms as they danced and when they drove home together.

While she danced and tried to smile and pretend to be happy, she felt heavy-hearted and guilty. She wasn't treating Keith fairly and she was deceiving her mother and her conscience was pricking her, but she refused to heed the gentle warning it gave her and she smiled her way through what seemed an endless evening. And again, she had no thought for Mark or what she was doing to him. She was only thinking of how she could use him to keep her from being lonely.

When Mark had driven her home and had left, she

turned to go inside. Then she heard the creaking of the porch swing. She was frightened, for she saw in the dim light at the end of the porch, someone sitting in the swing. She uttered a frightened gasp, then she heard a low laugh.

"Don't be afraid. It's no night prowler. But then I suppose I am a night prowler," he added.

She recognized Keith's voice and approached the swing. He held out his arms and she sat beside him and let him enfold her in his embrace.

"I couldn't go to sleep without seeing you, even if you didn't want me," he said tenderly as she held up her face for his kiss.

"I'm so glad you're not angry with me," she told him when there was time for talk again. "I didn't want to hurt you, but I couldn't do what you asked. I was miserable the whole evening. Every time I danced I was wishing it were you who was dancing with me."

"And I was writhing with jealousy, thinking of you being held in some other fellow's arms," he replied. "I don't know how I'm going to stand it, being away from you for so long, knowing that you'll be going somewhere so often with someone else, especially if it's with Mark."

"Why especially with Mark?" she asked with pretended ignorance.

"You know why. He's in love with you and he'll do all in his power to make you fall in love with him. And your mother will do all in her power to help him along," he said morosely.

"Then you don't trust me," she accused, pouting.

"I don't trust human nature," he stated. "When a fellow as good-looking and as acceptable as Mark is, and when your mother does everything in her power to influence you to like him and when I'm out of the picture for so long, it would be easy for you to fall in love with him and forget me."

"Please believe me. No matter how much my mother might try to influence me, and no matter how attractive Mark is or how he might try to win my love, I'll never stop loving you. When you come home and we're married, I'll have had my fun and I'll be satisfied to settle down and be a faithful wife and to raise a family if we should be fortunate enough to have one."

"The same old excuse," he remarked with a smile as he bent down and kissed her again. "I suppose I'll have to be satisfied to just wait and hope for the best."

"I'm still so young, Keith," she said seriously. "I wouldn't want to be married for a while even if you didn't have to leave. I've seen too many marriages that went on the rocks when youngsters got married and then were sorry when it was too late. I want our marriage to be one that will last as long as we live. If I've had my time of fun, I'll be ready for us to get married as soon as you want me when you return."

"I'll hold you to that promise, miss," he said as he put his cheek against hers and held her close.

Finally the day came for Keith's examination and he felt that he had been delivered from a gruelling period when it was at last over and he received his grades. He felt justified for all the time he had spent when he learned that he had made the highest marks in the group.

Faith rejoiced with him, but beneath all the joy over his success was the knowledge that in just a week or so he would be on his way to a base on the west coast.

The day before Keith was to leave, he was invited to dinner at Faith's home. Her father had suggested it, for he suspected that Faith was in love with Keith and in his heart he was glad, for he liked Keith and knew what a fine boy he was.

When they were alone in the swing on the porch a little before he had to leave, Keith pulled out a little box and opened it. In the dim light Faith could see that there was a large diamond, beautifully set and her heart gave a sudden leap.

"It's lovely!" she exclaimed as he held it toward her so that she might get a better look at it.

"May I put it on your finger, girl of my dreams?" he asked.

"Oh, Keith, I don't know," she said breathlessly.

"You know what I promised my mother. What will she think of me if she knows that I've broken my promise?"

"Why not tell her the truth?" he asked, taking her hand and slipping the ring on her finger while she looked down at it in admiration.

"I can't tell her the truth," she insisted. "I couldn't bear it. It'll be hard enough with you away, but if I have to see her disappointment in me and her hurt because I've broken my promise, it will make it a hundred times harder to bear. I can't wear it, Keith, much as I want to. I'd be proud to wear your ring, if it wasn't for that, but please don't ask me to do that to her."

"Wear it for tonight," he said, trying to hide his disappointment. "And sometimes when you think of me, slip it on and wear it for a little while, just to remember your promise and that I'll be believing that you will be true. Will you do that?"

"I will," she promised, while tears began to fill her eyes. "But I won't need that to remind me to be true."

He held her close while he bent down and kissed her.

"I'll have to say good-by, my darling," he murmured. "May God keep you and me while we're away from one another."

She sat there as he got his car started and left her, then she held up the ring and stared at it in the dim light. Her tears fell upon it, dimming its luster. She bent down and put her lips upon the wet stone, then wiped it carefully and put it back in the box.

She went to her room and put the ring in the back of her dresser drawer. A sigh escaped her. The months stretched ahead before her as a long, lonesome road. There was nothing in her heart but ache and longing. There was no hope, no comfort, for there was no one to whom she could go for comfort.

6

Faith opened her eyes the next morning upon a dreary world, rain-soaked, with heavy, scudding clouds. The trees were dripping from the rain which had come down in torrents during the night. Even the birds looked dismal and droopy as they sat upon the telephone wire leading to the house. They were water-soaked and they didn't seem to have the energy to shake themselves and preen their feathers.

Her spirits were in tune with the weather. The future looked as dismal as the morning outside. She got out of bed slowly and listlessly and began to dress. Until now, each day had held the promise of the joy of life, unexpected pleasures, but most of all, the assurance that she would see Keith or hear from him if they couldn't be together.

Until now, she had enjoyed making him jealous by accepting the attentions of others, especially Mark, for there was always the little happy time of reconciliation when she had assured him that it was he and he alone who held her heart in his keeping, that he would always have all there was of her love. Today there was no Keith and it would probably be a long time before she even had a letter from him.

She was sorry now that she had ever made him unhappy,

just for the fun of it. She regretted every flippant reply she had made when he had reproached her playing with him as she had so often done. If she only had him back again! She would never give him a moment's doubt of her love.

When she joined her parents for breakfast, they noticed how blue she was and they surmised the reason. Her mother said nothing. She thought the least said would be the best, but her father tried to cheer her up with a little word that might make her laugh. Instead it did the opposite. When he jokingly urged her to be the same little sunshine that she had always been and to look for a brighter tomorrow, she burst into tears and left the room until she could dry her eyes and eat her breakfast.

"You shouldn't have said anything," his wife admonished. "The less said, the better it will be for her. She'll have to live it down and if we sympathize with her, it'll only make matters worse."

"Poor kid!" he remarked. "I was only trying to make her smile a little. I know how she must feel. I feel so sorry for her. I know how much she must care for Keith."

His wife said nothing. She was trying to feel sorry for Faith, but she was glad that Keith would be out of the picture perhaps long enough for Faith to forget her love for him.

The meal was finished rather silently, for Faith was trying to keep back the tears and her parents didn't seem to have any desire for conversation.

Faith tried to read to pass the time until the weather cleared and she could go out, but couldn't become interested in what she was trying to read. She turned on the TV, but there was nothing that interested her. Finally she went to her room and prepared to get out her raincoat.

She told her mother that she thought she'd go over and see her friend Amy Southern. She paused a moment before her dresser as she passed it on her way to the closet where her raincoat hung and she opened the top drawer. She took the ring out and looked at it. It was more beautiful in the light of day than it had been in the dim light last night. It must have cost a lot of money, she thought, for the diamond was large and there were other little diamonds in the setting. She slipped it on and admired it while tears gathered in her eyes.

How she wished that she could wear it! She would be so happy and so proud to let the world know that she had promised herself to Keith, even if it meant that the other boys would leave her alone. But she couldn't hurt her mother by letting her know that she had broken her promise. She knew that when her mother learned the truth, she would be disappointed, but she wanted to put off that day until she could no longer keep the truth from her. If Keith hadn't had to go away, she would have let her know the truth, but now it was different.

She put her lips to the diamond again, then put it back in its box and hid it among her handkerchiefs at the back of the drawer.

As she kissed her mother good-by, her mother said, "Try to be happy, darling. It makes my heart ache to know that yours is aching. All I want in the world is your happiness."

"Thanks, Mom," Faith answered through trembling lips. "I'll try not to be a gloom spreader, but just give me time. I'll be back for lunch."

As she walked toward Amy's house, she saw the little sparrows sitting disconsolately on the fence with their wet feathers drooping.

"You look just like I feel," she remarked.

One of them darted a swift look at her, then flew away and the others followed.

"I wish that I too could fly away, little birds," she called to them. "I'd fly right out to that west coast base and beg Keith to take me with him, no matter what the rules and regulations were."

Amy greeted her with a kiss as she let Faith in.

"I know how you feel," she remarked. "I feel the same way. Johnny will be gone at noon. He just phoned me and told me good-by. I could cry my eyes out."

"Then we'll have a good time crying together," Faith remarked as her spirits lifted a little. They both laughed.

"I told Mother that Johnny and I are engaged," Amy said. "I told her that I'd wait for him, no matter how long I might have to wait. She knows that I'm too young to marry now and I think she's glad that Johnny is out of the way for a while at least, but she's willing, when he comes home — if he ever comes home," and a little sob escaped her.

"Of course he'll come home," Faith stated. "Why shouldn't he? He's only in training."

"He'll be going overseas in a short time, when he finishes his basic training," Amy argued. "They'll be going on test flights and almost every day we read of some kind of accident to our planes. I believe it's sabotage. Johnny might just be unfortunate enough to be in one of those planes."

"Goodness! I never thought of that," Faith exclaimed in a weak little voice. "I never even thought that something might happen to Keith."

"I know you're in love with each other and I'm sure you must be engaged to him. Aren't you?" Amy asked.

They had kept few things from each other, for they had been close friends ever since they were children.

"I promised my mother that there would be nothing between us until he returned," Faith evaded.

She couldn't let Amy know how she had deceived her mother.

"Just the same, I know that in your heart you belong to him. Just don't let Mark and those other boys make you forget him," Amy advised. "I know they would like to, especially Mark. He's been trying to take you away from Keith for a long time."

"He'll never succeed in doing that," Faith assured her.

By trying to comfort each other, they were happier and their spirits received a lift, just to know that someone else was in the same slough of despond. However, as Faith left Amy, her heart bore a heavier burden. It had not occurred to her that Keith might be in danger. She had just thought that he would serve his time in training and then be released to come home. Now she would have the fear that something might happen to him. If such a catastrophe should happen, she would want to die, for she wouldn't want to live without him.

Now that he was gone, she loved him more than ever. She had always taken him for granted, but now there was the danger that he might never come back to her. She grew cold with fear as she thought of that possibility, but she tried to put that horrible thought out of her mind.

When she greeted her mother, she tried to look more cheerful and her mother remarked about it.

"I'm glad to see that smile in your eyes again," she remarked. "Now you look like my little girl always looked. It was good for you to see Amy."

"We enjoyed talking about our mutual sorrows," Faith replied with a twisted little smile. "Johnny left for the East today. We're both war widows now."

"Not for long, though," her mother answered with an encouraging smile.

Mark phoned that afternoon and asked Faith if he could take her for dinner and a little ride afterward. She didn't want to go and at first she hesitated to accept his invitation, but the prospect of sitting around home all evening with nothing to do but look at TV and think of Keith, was more than she could face, so she told him that she would go with him.

When she told her mother, her mother tried not to reveal how happy she was as she said that it would be good for her to get away from home.

"Mark's a real friend in need," she remarked. "I'm sure that he knows how lonely you'll be with Keith away. It's thoughtful of him to want to help you not to be too lonesome."

"I appreciate his thoughtfulness," Faith replied.

She knew that Mark's invitation was not mere thoughtful friendship. He was taking this early opportunity to take Keith's place, if he could. She knew that he was in love with her and was determined to get what he wanted. She was willing to accept his attentions, even though she knew that she would be encouraging him when there was no hope for him. She was willing to do anything or go anywhere with anyone who asked her, if it would help her bear her loneliness and her longing for Keith.

Though Mark suspected her reason for accepting his invitation, he gave no hint of his suspicions when he came for her. Later on, during the evening, he mentioned Keith and he remarked that he was sure that Faith would miss him.

"I know that old Keith will miss you much more than you'll miss him," he added with a smile.

"What makes you think that?" she asked.

"Because he'll be in boot camp and he knows no girls, while you'll be here surrounded with friends who'll do everything to make you forget your loneliness. And perhaps to forget him," he added.

"Will that be kind of all of you?" she asked. "Keith and I are good friends like we've always been and it would be hard for anyone to make me forget a friend."

"No one should forget a friend," he agreed. "I hope that I shall prove to be such a good friend that you will at least let me do my utmost to make you happy while he's gone."

"You're very kind, friend," she said with a smile. "I'll appreciate your every effort to make me happy. That's just what I want to be, happy. If you can do that, then you're a whiz."

"I'll show you what a great whiz I can be," he said jokingly.

"Go right ahead and do your stuff." she laughed.

"Then may I take you to the dance at the yacht club next week?" he asked.

"Don't rush me," she warned. "Give me time to think. I had told Keith that I would go with him, but the telegram arrived right after we had made our plans. I'll let you know. I'll probably say yes, unless there's someone else whom you would want to ask."

"There is no one else. There never will be," he said. Then he changed the subject.

She appreciated his tact in doing this, for she was in no mood to listen to any of the things he had said on other occasions.

She knew before she went to bed that she would go with him to that dance. She couldn't sit at home and think of what would be happening if Keith had been there and they had been together. She must do everything she could to forget her loneliness, but nothing could ever make her forget her love for Keith. She was convinced of that.

7

On the night of the dance Faith's mother was pleased to observe that Faith was excited at the prospect of another evening's outing. She had noticed during the intervening days that Faith had been more cheerful and she hoped that Faith was beginning to become accustomed to Keith's absence and was making the best of it.

When Mark arrived, Faith was glowing and beautiful. The eager light in her eyes rejoiced her mother even more.

When they arrived at the club, there were many others already there and a buzz of conversation greeted them when they entered. As soon as the boys of her acquaintance saw her, they came and asked for a dance and her card was soon filled. It was the custom at these formal dances to have cards and there was no cutting in allowed.

Mark was annoyed that he hadn't had the foresight to have reserved more dances for himself, though he tried to conceal his annoyance and his jealousy.

Faith had to acknowledge to herself when the dance was over, that she'd had a wonderful time. She had not had time to think of Keith very often. Once or twice when a familiar number was played, one of those that had been their favorite, she thought of him and a little wave of longing swept over her, but it soon passed as she danced and listened to the conversation of her partner.

"I hope now that Keith is out of the way for a spell, you'll give the rest of us a chance," one of her partners said as they swung through the rhythm of a waltz. There were no modern dances in this select group.

"There never was any reason why Keith should have kept us from being friends while he was here, so why shouldn't we be friends, now that he's gone?" she asked. "I'm glad that you want to be friends, for I shall miss him. We've been friends for so long."

"I'm not thinking of friendship and you know it," he said, giving her a look that made his meaning quite clear.

"Let's leave it at that for the present," she advised. "Just now, the only thing I want is friendship. I don't want to be serious for a long time yet."

"You mean until Keith comes back," he retorted.

"No matter what I mean, let's just be friends for now. That's the way I'd rather have it."

"But you will give me a chance to be more than a friend some day, won't you?" he persisted.

"Perhaps, but don't rush me."

She was exhilarated and happy over the attention that she received and she felt that, after all, she might be able to bear it while Keith was away.

"I didn't have much of a chance tonight," Mark remarked when they were on their way home. "I was stupid not to have clinched more of those dances for myself."

"I think it was very unselfish of you to give someone else the chance to renew old acquaintance," she told him with a little smile.

"Renew old acquaintance, my eye! That's a neat way to put it, but I won't grumble. I'll just hope that they keep out of my way, for I don't expect to give them many more chances to renew old acquaintance in the future."

"Now you're being selfish," she said with pretended severity.

45

"Selfish or not, that's the way it'll be if I can manage it," he replied. "You know the old saying, 'All's fair in love and war!' "

"I might ask which this is, but I'd rather not know. At least not tonight. I've had such a wonderful time that I don't want it spoiled by hints of war."

He laughed. "Nor by thoughts of love, I suppose."

"You're right," she said seriously.

"Then we'll not mention either. I want only what you want. You know that."

There was a warm note in his voice which she couldn't mistake, but she ignored it and he changed the subject.

During the week or so following, he called her every day and talked to her for a while. "Just to keep you from forgetting me," he explained.

When he asked her for another dinner date, she didn't hesitate, but accepted. She confessed to herself that she enjoyed being with him and she didn't care if she was leading him on by encouraging him and by accepting dates with him.

Days passed and she didn't hear from Keith. At first she didn't worry, for she knew that there would be much that he would have to do to get adjusted to his new life and routine, but as the days passed, she was surprised, then she was hurt and after that she was worried and afraid that something had happened to him.

When at last she did hear, her worries were relieved. He wrote that he had been ill for a while and that he had had no opportunity to write even a note.

"When you're in sick bay, you're in and that's that," he wrote. "It was some of the shots that did the damage, I suppose, but then we're not told much. We only know that we're sick and that the doctors are doing their best to get us well and back in training."

He mentioned something of the rigorous training they were having and that, though it seemed pretty rough, it was what they needed to put them in shape for whatever they might have to meet.

"I think of you every waking hour," he wrote at the close of his letter, "and I dream of you so very often. I'm just existing until the day I may see you again."

Her spirits soared. To be assured that he still cared and hadn't found someone else and that nothing serious had happened to him, was all she needed to make her happy. She never considered how unfair she was being to Keith and to Mark. She was thinking only of herself, what she could do to enjoy herself while Keith was away, no matter how much others might be hurt.

Mark was invited to dinner more often and Faith's mother rejoiced to observe how much he seemed to enjoy being with them. She still hoped that Faith would follow the religion of her ancestors. It might atone in a measure for her own lapse.

She remembered that in the prayers which were offered in the synagogue, these prayers were not solely for the sins of the ones who offered them, but they were offered for all others of like faith who might have sinned and wandered from the true way.

Only by marrying Mark would Faith have the opportunity to become a true descendant of Abraham. Then she too could pray for her mother's sins, something which she herself couldn't do, since she was no longer an observer of the laws and the services of her own people.

One evening when Faith and Mark were dining out and they were driving afterward, he asked her a question that surprised her.

"Would you do something for me, if I asked you?" he began. "It means a lot to me."

"I will, if I can," she replied, hesitating. "What is it?"

"Would you go with me to the synagogue service Friday night? It would make me very happy if you would go."

"I don't know," Faith told him. "Of course you know that my mother doesn't follow her religion. I'm sure that your mother knows that."

"Yes, she did mention it once," he admitted. "But I know that your mother would be happy if you would go with

47

me. I know that in her heart she is still a true Jew. She can never get away from that. Will you go with me? Please say yes."

"Give me time to think," she asked. "I'll let you know."

"Thanks," he replied. "I shall be waiting and hoping."

8

Faith wondered what she should do about going with Mark. She wanted to please him and she knew that if she went with him, it would please her mother, but she wondered what Keith would think if he knew that she had gone. He might think that she was leaning toward her mother's faith and she thought that this might worry him, for she knew that his mother wanted him to follow her belief. She also wondered how her father would feel.

She remembered how her father had taken her to Sunday school in his church. That was when she was too young to understand the situation between her parents concerning their religious differences. She wondered if it would displease him. She wanted to please her mother, but she didn't want to hurt him, for she loved him very much and sometimes she felt closer to her father than she did to her mother. She used to wonder why he never went to church until she grew old enough to understand that neither of them followed their beliefs.

She wondered if it was of any real importance, whether she should settle the whole disquieting problem by telling Mark that she'd rather not go with him. But she was afraid that if she did this, it might displease Mark's mother — and that she wouldn't want Mark to continue their friendship. His mother was a strict orthodox Jewess.

She knew that Mark's father was in business of his own and that he did not observe the Jewish Sabbath by closing his place of business. How could he justify breaking his Sabbath law by working on that day, she wondered. Perhaps she'd ask Mark about this sometime. He always seemed pleased whenever she asked him anything about his religion.

She thought she knew why this pleased him. He was hoping that she would become a true Jewess and follow her mother's religion. She finally decided that she would speak to her mother and then make her decision as to what she should do. How she wished that Mark had not asked her to go, for it presented an upsetting problem. Religion was something that was never discussed in her family and she now understood the reason.

When she told her mother what Mark had asked and asked her what she should do, her mother's eyes filled with tears. They were tears of joy.

"I don't want to hurt him by refusing," Faith said, "and I don't want to hurt Dad, if he wouldn't want me to go, but I'm sure you would be happy if I did, wouldn't you?" and a little smile hovered upon her lips.

"It would indeed make me happy," her mother told her. "You've never had the opportunity to see what our service is like and perhaps you've forgotten what it was like in your father's church."

"I never went to a church service, only to Sunday school," Faith said. "I never knew why Dad stopped taking me when I grew old enough to sit through a church service."

Her mother didn't enlighten her upon that subject.

"I think I'd like to go, if it wouldn't hurt Dad," Faith finally said.

She didn't tell her mother that she still wondered what Keith would think if he knew that she had gone with Mark.

She decided that she would speak to her father before she gave Mark his answer.

"I want you to tell me how you would really feel if I went," she said.

"Is just one visit of so much importance?" he asked. "It might do you good if you would visit some of the other churches and find out just what they teach."

"I'm not really interested in what any of them believe or what they teach," she told him. "I like Mark and I don't want him to be angry with me if I don't go. That's the only reason I would like to go if it doesn't hurt you. I know it would please his mother if I should go. That's all I want to do, please them both. I know his mother might not like the idea of his going steady with me, for she knows that I'm not truly Jewish and she is very orthodox."

"Are you in love with Mark, baby?" he asked tenderly. "Is that why you're so anxious to please him?"

"I'm not in love with him, but I do like him a lot. He's been so nice to me since Keith went away and I'd be lonely without him. The other boys have sort of stayed away and left the field open to him. I'd be left high and dry if he, too, dropped me."

He smiled tenderly at her. "You wouldn't be dropped for long, honey. You're too beautiful to sit on the side lines for long. But tell me one thing. Are you in love with Keith? I believe you are. I've seen the signs for a long time. I've been wondering if you've forgotten him since Mark has been paying you so much attention."

"I promised Mom that I wouldn't make Keith any promise until he gets out of the service," she evaded.

"But that doesn't keep you from loving him. Tell me, honey, how is it with you two?"

"I love him, Daddy, very much," and she sighed. "I was wondering what he would think and how he would feel if he knew that I went with Mark."

"I shouldn't think it would make any great difference to him," he stated. "He knows that, since you're not engaged to him, you'll be going with other boys while he's away and he'll want you to be happy. I think he can trust you as much as you would trust him. So don't make such an issue of this little

51

trifle and go with the young man if you want to."

She kissed him on his cheek and murmured, "Thank you, Daddy. You're such a comfort."

She felt guilty as she left him, for she had deceived him also.

He sighed as she left him. Had he ever given her the right kind of comfort? He knew that he himself was a failure as far as spiritual truths were concerned and he felt that he had failed in the most important decision of his life. But he tossed the painful thought aside as his wife joined him.

"Do you think you're being fair to Keith, dear, when you encourage Mark to take such complete possession of Faith's time?" he asked.

"I haven't said anything to Faith to make her encourage Mark," she replied. "What makes you ask that? I've let her make her own decision as to what she should do. I only asked her to wait until Keith came home before she made any promise to him and she said she would."

"About this visit to the synagogue with Mark. I know it would please you if she would go with him. Did you tell her that?"

"Yes, I did," she admitted. "You know what I've always hoped, though we agreed not to influence her one way or another. I've hoped that she would follow my faith when she grew old enough to choose for herself. It might atone for the sorrow that I caused my mother and the bitterness that my father held against me even to his death. But I've kept the promise we both made not to try to influence her one way or the other."

"I've hoped that she would one day follow the faith that my mother had," he said with a sorrowful note in his voice. "I haven't been as true to what my mother taught me as you have to your belief, for I've never become what she prayed that I would become, a true believer in her Saviour who should have been mine.

"I know that we agreed never to argue about the difference in our beliefs and I've tried to keep the decision we both made. I remember that when Faith was old enough to begin to ask questions about what she heard in Sunday school and you asked me not to take her any more, I stopped taking her. I feel that then is where I forsook even the influence of my own faith because I loved you so much that I never wanted to cause you a moment's unhappiness."

"We've both paid a terrible price for the love we had for each other," she said sadly. "Sometimes I wonder if we did the right thing in causing so many heartaches. I wonder if God will punish us for it."

"Are you sorry for what we did?" he asked, a note of pain in his voice.

"No. I can't be sorry, even though I wonder what the end will be, even though there still remains a weight of guilt on my heart. I could never regret that I married you, for the love I have for you outweighs everything else, even that feeling of guilt."

He took her in his arms and held her for a moment, then he bent and kissed her.

"You're the only thing in life that counts with me," he said brokenly. "Your love and your child and mine are all that I have in the world. I pray that somehow God will work things so that He will take away our burden of guilt and let us be completely happy before the end comes to us."

"I, too, pray that that may happen," she whispered as she put her arms around his neck and drew his lips to hers.

Both of them prayed for the mercy of a God whom neither of them served or honored in the only way that God required of them. And they prayed to a God whom they did not really know or love, for they had never committed their lives to Him who was only a name to them.

9

Mark was hoping that Faith would be impressed by the service, for he was also hoping that she would accept the faith of her fathers. According to his religious law, the child became what her mother was and since Faith's mother was a Jew, he knew that in his religion, Faith was already one, even though she did not believe.

Mark's mother had had a long talk with him when she knew that he was paying so much attention to Faith. She was both disappointed and worried. Above everything else, when he married, she had hoped that the girl would be a true Jew.

"But Faith is really a Jew," he insisted when his mother had told him how she felt and had asked him not to go with Faith so often. "Her mother is an orthodox Jew, even though she married a Gentile," he argued.

"I know that," his mother replied, "but when she married, she broke her mother's heart and her father disowned her. And Faith's father broke his mother's heart because he didn't follow her religion and because he married a Jewish girl."

"How did you know that?" he asked surprised.

"From someone I've known for years, who knew the

whole story. She was the one who told me that you were going steady with Faith.''

''She's an old meddler,'' Mark exclaimed. ''She's just trying to stir up trouble and she's succeeded.''

''She was thinking of me,'' his mother corrected. ''She thought I should know so that I might do something that would keep you from doing what would bring sorrow to both of us.

''Are you in love with this girl?'' she asked when Mark was silent.

''Yes, I am,'' he declared.

''Give her up, son, unless you want to break my heart too,'' she begged.

''I can't do that, Mother,'' he said, shaking his head. ''I don't know whether she loves me or not. I'm afraid she's in love with Keith Loring, but I hope that she will care for me, now that he's gone.''

''Then I shall pray to God that she won't fall in love with you,'' she said.

''Perhaps I can win her to our religion,'' he offered. ''She's nothing now. She told me that. If she'll become a Jewish believer, won't that make a difference? Won't you be willing for me to try to win her? I hate to say this, and I don't want to hurt you, Mother, but I won't stop trying to win her love. I'll do everything I can to win her to our religion so that you'll be happy, but I can't give up the hope of winning her love. I'll ask her to go with me to a service. If she'll go, then perhaps everything will turn out all right for both of us. Will you be willing to let me try?''

''Of course,'' she told him, but she hoped that Faith would refuse to go with him. She had little hope that the girl would turn to her mother's religion after all these years. But perhaps, if she loved Mark enough, she might even do that. She could only wait and hope.

Mark decided that he would not take Faith to the service where the men and women were seated separately, for he was afraid that this would hinder his efforts and that she wouldn't want to come again.

Since it was the first time Faith had ever been inside a synagogue, she looked around her with interest. She remembered the simple arrangement of the church she had attended. The inside of this sanctuary was more elaborate.

She noticed that as they entered the synagogue, Mark slipped out a little black skull cap and put it on his head. All the other men wore these same caps.

Before her, at the far end of the sanctuary, she saw a stand or pulpit upon the platform. At the other side there was a receptacle. While she was wondering what these two represented, the speaker went to the receptacle, above which a light was burning, and took out some scrolls from which he began to read.

The congregation joined him as he began to chant certain prayers and passages from the Psalms. Since she was not familiar with the Psalms, she couldn't understand the words and this bored her though she tried to listen attentively.

She tried to become interested in the service and in the long and somewhat tiresome message of the rabbi, but she was glad when the service was over and they were on their way for a short ride before Mark took her home.

"How did you like the service?" he asked hopefully. "Wasn't it impressive?"

"I can't say that it was," she confessed. "I didn't understand what most of it was all about. I couldn't catch the words of the chants and I wondered about some of the things I saw there. For instance, why was that little receptacle over to one side and not out in front beside the speaker's stand?"

"That little receptacle is the ark of the Covenant that is in all orthodox synagogues. When God gave Moses the Law and the tabernacle was built in the wilderness, the ark was in the Holy of Holies. We keep the Pentateuch, that is, the books of the Law, in that little ark to remind us that Moses received the Law from God."

"Why does it have that light above it?" she asked.

"That is the perpetual light that signifies the indestructible flame of religion. The ark is placed so that when a person faces it, he is facing toward Jerusalem. In the story of

Daniel we read that he always prayed facing the land of his fathers, where Jerusalem stood."

"You surely do know your Bible," she remarked.

"Don't you read your Gentile Bible?" he asked.

"No, I've never seen one in our home. I think that my father must have had one, but my father and mother agreed not to try to influence me in their religious faith, so I suppose he put his Bible away where I never saw it."

If she had known her Bible and if he had known his Old Testament as it had been written and not superimposed by man's tradition, both would have known that everything in the tabernacle in the wilderness was a type of the Christ, whom neither of them knew. They would have realized that though the synagogue had some of the furniture that brought to mind the tabernacle and the furnishings, their spiritual significance was lost through the failure of the people to believe in the One to whose coming all Old Testament Scripture pointed, the One who had come and whom they had rejected. They would have understood that that eternal flame typified Christ, the Light of the world, and not the "indestructible flame of religion."

"I'd love to help you understand more about our religion, if you'll let me," he offered hopefully.

"I would like to know more about it," she admitted. "I know that my mother would be pleased if she knew that I was interested in her religion. I don't think it matters one way or another to my father. He once said that all of us were trying to get to heaven one way or another and it didn't matter so much which way we took, just so we got there. He said that, of course, no one wanted to go to hell."

"We don't believe in hell," he asserted.

"You don't!" she exclaimed. "I thought everyone believed in hell. That's why I get afraid sometimes when I wonder where I'd go if I die."

"The word hell is only mentioned in the New Testament. The word in our Scriptures is Sheol and that means a place where the dead just lead a colorless existence and wait for removal to a happier place. After a person dies, he is finally purged from his sins and grows spiritually until he reaches a happier existence.''

She was silent. In her memory she recalled a lesson she had heard when she was attending Sunday school. Her teacher had said that Jesus was a Saviour who had come to earth to die on a cross and shed His blood so that even little children could be saved from sin and go to heaven and not have to go to hell.

The very word had filled her with fear. She had asked her mother about it and told how afraid she was of that terrible place. It was after that that her father had stopped taking her to Sunday school. It was then that her mother had begun a feeble attempt to indoctrinate Faith in the Jewish belief, but her efforts had only served to confuse the girl more and she lost interest in both beliefs.

''I suppose that is a very comforting belief,'' she remarked. ''It's much better to believe that we can be forgiven of our sins and go on to a higher place than to be kept in hell forever because of some little sin.''

Neither of them realized how wrong they were. Mark was happy because she seemed interested and she was satisfied to accept what he had told her, for it made little difference to her. Her spiritual life didn't concern her at present. Just now she was thinking of Keith and yearning for a sight of him, yearning to be held in his arms once more and to feel his lips warm against hers.

When they reached her home, Mark turned to her and his voice was warm and pleading.

''Faith, you must know that I love you. I'd give anything in the world if you would just say you care a little and it would be the happiest day of my life if you would accept the faith of your ancestors and become a true Jew. It would make Mother so happy and I know that it would also make your mother happy. I promised not to say anything about love for a while at least, but I can't keep silent any longer. Will you give me just a little encouragement and say that you do care a little?''

''I do care a lot, Mark,'' she replied, ''but I can't say

that I love you. Let's leave it that way for now. Give me time. I want your mother and my mother to be happy, and I'll try to believe that you want me to, but just now I'm all confused.

I want to do the right thing. I really do. Please wait and give me time."

He put his arms around her and held her though she wanted to release herself.

"I'll never give up hope, my dearest," he murmured.

He tried to kiss her, but she turned her face away and he kissed her on her cheek.

"Won't you let me kiss you just this once?" he begged. "I won't ask for more."

She let him kiss her and his lips clung to hers long and ardently. She knew that she was being unfaithful to Keith and that she was not being fair to Mark, but she didn't care. She wanted release from loneliness and she thought that this was the only way out.

When Mark left her his heart was singing and his hopes were high, while she went to her room feeling more like a traitor and a deceiver than ever. Now she had added Mark to her list. She had deceived her mother and her father and had broken faith with Keith, but she went to sleep without the thought of prayer and she didn't let her conscience worry her. She had stilled it's voice so often that it seldom spoke to her. When it did, as the still small voice, she refused to listen, while she tried to justify herself in whatever she was doing.

10

At the first opportunity Faith's mother asked her how she enjoyed her visit to the synagogue. Faith was hoping that she wouldn't ask, for she didn't know how to answer her.

"I can't say that I enjoyed it," she was forced to confess. "It was all so strange and I couldn't understand the chants. I thought the sanctuary was very attractive. I couldn't understand the words when they were chanting and the rabbi talked so long that I got tired. All he talked about was Israel's past glory and their duty to keep the Law and to look for the coming of the Messiah. How could that help anyone to live a better life today?"

"You'd soon understand, if you'd keep going," her mother assured her. "Perhaps this message wasn't suited to what you had expected to hear. He speaks upon many subjects, some of them to educate the people and others are to remind them of the past and the future glory of our people."

"I suppose I just didn't know enough to understand," Faith conceded.

As the fall season approached, the most important Jewish holidays drew near. Mark was hoping that Faith would go with him to their most important services. He thought that if she would continue to go, she would understand and better appreciate just what it meant to be a true Jew. He knew that her mother would do all she could to help Faith to become interested in her religion, now that she had made the first step in that direction.

He was right, for her mother did all she could without seeming to press her daughter to make a decision. She tried to give her some of the teachings that she herself had known for so long. She even read certain passages from the Psalms, which Faith didn't know that she possessed.

Faith tried to appear interested, but she wasn't really. Her mind and heart were closed to anything that pertained to the spiritual life. She had lived too long without any spiritual instruction.

Though Mark's mother still hoped that he would transfer his attentions to some girl who was more firmly fixed in her Jewish faith, she was friendly to Faith and invited her to dinner. Faith was pleased and surprised, though she thought she knew the reason for the invitation.

Mark's mother was gracious and entertaining and Faith enjoyed the evening as well as the delicious food.

Faith's father saw what was happening and his conscience began to trouble him even more. He remembered his mother and how she had yearned over him and prayed for him. As he thought of how miserably he had failed her and his child, he decided to do something about it. He spoke to his wife about it.

"I don't think you're playing fair with me," he told her. "You're doing everything in your power to influence Faith to become a Jew when we promised to do differently."

"We said we'd leave it to her to make her own decision about that," his wife argued. "She's old enough to make up her own mind now about what she wants to do."

"But you're trying to help her make up her mind," he accused. "You've made her understand how it pleased you when she went to that synagogue service and you're letting Mark help you to make up her mind."

"Can I help it if she likes him and if she's willing to go

with him to his place of worship?" she asked in hurt tones.

"Maybe not, but neither are you hindering her," and he gave her a smile. "I'm not quarreling, just wondering. I realize what we both passed through in our love and marriage and I want to be very sure that she's making the right choice before she turns Keith down and takes Mark. I'm going to ask her if she'll go to church with me this coming Sunday."

"I have no objections," she told him and the subject was closed.

When he asked Faith if she would go with him, she gave him a roguish smile.

"You're trying to keep me from becoming a Jew," she accused.

"I'm trying to let you see both sides of our religious beliefs," he said. "Now that you're old enough to make up your own mind, I want you to have a chance to see both sides before you make a decision which one you want to follow."

"I'm not sure that I want to follow either one," she said. "I'm happy just as I am. If Keith were just here, I'd be too happy to bother about anything else. I'd just be with him and that would be all I want."

"Then you're not in love with Mark," her father said in a relieved tone.

"No, Daddy, I'm not," she said. "I love Keith, but I do like Mark and I want to please him as long as he's nice to me."

"Then how about church?"

"Of course I'll go with you," and she gave him a kiss.

Faith's mother watched them as they left for church and there was a prayer on her lips.

"God of my fathers," she murmured, "don't let her be misled by this heretical belief. May she become a true Jew and carry on the belief of our ancestors."

Perhaps the whole story might have been different if the pastor had been a man who was true to his calling, who was on fire for the Lord and for winning souls. His message was cold and uninteresting. He went at length into some passage of Corinthians dealing with corruption in the church and how it should be met in this present day congregation, and he castigated those who were indifferent about paying their pledges. Before he finished, he did manage to bring in the name of Christ, but it was when Christ rebuked the Pharisees for keeping the ceremonial law while they failed to obey the greater law of the new covenant.

Faith's father was terribly disappointed, for he knew that nothing had been accomplished. There had been nothing that could have made Faith want to accept this belief. There was nothing there that made him want to yield his heart to God in answer to his mother's prayers.

"We surely picked the wrong time to come," he remarked as they were on their way home. "That preacher wasn't up to standard today. I'm afraid he didn't help you much."

"I'm afraid he only confused me," she admitted. "When the rabbi preached, he dwelt upon the past glory of his people and he condemned all those who refused to believe in the God of Israel, while this preacher condemned the Pharisees when he quoted what Jesus of Nazareth said when He rebuked them. They're fighting each other."

"It surely looks that way," he replied morosely, disappointed.

"Don't worry, Daddy," she said, patting his arm as he drove. "I'm still neither Jew nor Gentile. I suppose I'm just a hybrid."

"Just stay that way," he advised, but he was unhappy over the situation.

When Mark asked her if she would go with him to the Shofar service, she said she would go. He had told her what a beautiful service it was and she knew that she would not be hurting her father by going and that her mother would be delighted. It was somewhere to go and there was no other place she could go that evening, for the other boys had deserted her.

Mark's parents went with them and she felt rather constrained as she sat beside Mark.

The service began with the blowing of the Shofar, the

63

trumpet made from a ram's horn. It commemorated the occasion when Moses received the Law at Mt. Sinai, accompanied by blasts from the Shofar. Again the Shofar was blown when Israel was commanded by God to resume their journey. After this the congregation began to chant from the Psalms. Some passages mentioned the hope that some day God's sovereignty over all people would be proclaimed by the blowing of the Shofar. She listened with more interest as the rabbi spoke of the time when all Israel would be gathered together again in the land which God had promised to Abraham.

As she listened, she thought that perhaps this was really the true religion after all and that all other beliefs were really only heresy, that these people who came from the same ancestry that she did, were really the chosen of God. She hated to think what her father would feel if she accepted her mother's religion instead of his.

She was not thinking of Keith just now. When, later on, she thought of him, she knew that it would make no difference to him what she believed. He had no real belief himself.

When Mark's mother asked her if she would go with them to the Kol Nidre service, she agreed to go. She wanted to learn more of the religion of her mother's people. She felt that her father was being neglected, but she couldn't help that. If she ever accepted any belief, that time was a long way off. There would be plenty of time for that later on.

At this sacred service, everyone entered the synagogue as if they were on tiptoe. There was scarcely a sound as the people took their seats and waited for the service to begin. The older men wore the Tellit, or white robes. The more strictly orthodox women wore white, while many others wore ordinary clothes. Mark's mother wore ordinary clothes, while Mark and his father put on their small black caps as they entered the sanctuary.

Faith had asked Mark about why they wore those caps and he had told her that the cap was called a yarmulke and that they were supposed to wear them when they were in the presence of God.

The service began with the opening of the ark when the scrolls were taken out. Then the cantor began to sing the famed Kol Nidre with its beautiful melody. The congregation joined in the prayer as the cantor repeated the song three times. This seemed to Faith to be more of a declaration than a prayer. Mrs. Ledbetter explained on the way home that it was a declaration to relieve them of all pledges that they had made and had not been able to keep. This dated from the time of the Spanish inquisition when thousands of Jews had been compelled to become Christians against their will. They made their vows openly, but followed their old customs in secret.

The next day Faith received a letter from Keith that made her spirits soar. She had received letters from him frequently after that first delay and each one had pricked her conscience as she realized how she was leading Mark along. She wondered what would happen if Keith came back and learned the truth.

Keith told her in this letter that he might be able to come home for Thanksgiving. He didn't say how long he would have, but just the prospect of seeing him even for a little while filled her with excitement and joy.

Her mother hoped that the change she saw in Faith after she had received the letter was because she had fallen in love with Mark. She didn't think it had anything to do with the letter, for Keith wrote so frequently that she didn't pay much attention. She didn't ask any questions and Faith didn't enlighten her. Faith decided not to mention the prospect of Keith's visit until he came, for she knew that problems might arise which she didn't want to face until she had to.

There was a paragraph in Keith's letter that filled her with curiosity. He wrote, "Something quite wonderful has happened to me, so wonderful that I don't want to write it, for I could never explain it in a letter. I'm so eager to tell you all about it. I'm hoping that one day it will mean as much to you as it has meant to me."

Her curiosity mounted as the days passed and her impatience grew with it, but she would have to wait until he came and the time seemed endless until then.

11

When Keith entered the training center on the west coast, his one desire was to finish his time of service and get back to Faith. He had no concern about spiritual facts, for he gave his spiritual condition no thought. He was even more indifferent than he had been, for he was associated with many who were in the same condition.

He had been billeted with Roger Mills, another young lieutenant in his same corps. Their first night together gave him a sudden shock. When they were ready for bed, before lights out, Roger took out a New Testament and began to read from it. When he had finished, he knelt beside his bunk and prayed.

Two others who were billeted with them looked on with smiles before they settled themselves to sleep. As Keith watched Roger praying, a feeling of guilt crept over him. Here was a fellow who wasn't ashamed to let others know that he honored God and His Word. Keith respected Roger for it. He knew that Roger would be in for a lot of ridicule from some of the others.

Keith felt ashamed of his own sin of unbelief, or rather, his failure to act upon what he really did believe. He remembered how his mother had told him before he left that if she should die while he was away, her last prayer would be for his salvation. He knew how grieved she had been because he had never accepted Christ as his Saviour.

As he lay there in the darkness, after Roger had gotten into bed, he wondered at himself, that he could have been so indifferent all this time, how he could resist the impulse to drop to his knees beside his mother as she said those words and pray to the Lord for forgiveness.

Deep within his heart he knew that it had been his love for Faith that had kept him from answering the call of the Holy Spirit to yield his heart and life to the Lord. He knew that Faith's mother didn't approve of him, because he was not a Jew. If he really were a devoted Christian and insisted upon being true to his faith, she would be even more opposed. He decided to put off any decision until he and Faith were married.

As he fell asleep with these disturbing thoughts upon his mind, his sleep was a troubled one. He decided that he'd steer clear of Roger, much as he liked him from their first meeting, for he didn't want to be disturbed by too close association with him. Roger would discover how far he was from God and he might try to persuade him to accept the Lord, and Keith wanted none of that. He had a job to do for his country and a girl waiting for him when that job was finished — that was all he wanted in life just now.

It didn't take Roger long to discover that Keith was avoiding him and he wondered if he had guessed the reason why. He knew that Keith wasn't a Christian. He was having his share of ridicule, for the two who shared their quarters soon let it be known that he was a Christian fellow and they gave him such jibes as only a group like this could give.

He took it good naturedly and replied to their questions that were asked only to get a laugh from the others. Often his answers put them to shame, for he not only answered their silly questions, but he told them in his quiet way, just what he believed and why he believed it. Finally they became ashamed of themselves and ceased to torment him. They began to respect his courage in standing up for what he believed, even though they had no desire to accept it as theirs.

Keith stood on the side lines when the others ridiculed Roger. As the days passed, his respect grew with that of the others and finally he no longer tried to avoid Roger, but sought his friendship again.

"You've got a lot of courage," he told Roger one day when they were on their way from drill. "I'd have pitched into those guys and given them a beating or else, for the things they've been doing to you."

"Maybe they wouldn't have been the ones who got the beating," Roger replied with a smile. "I might have been snowed under myself if I had tried it." Then, seriously, "I'll confess that I might have had the inclination to answer them as they deserved to be answered, for they said some pretty nasty things, but I prayed before I came here that the Lord would give me the grace to stand true to Him, no matter what. I knew what would happen that first night when I knelt down to pray, for I knew that none of you were Christians, or you would have been there on your knees with me. You see, I not only prayed for myself, but I knew that I had a mother at home who was praying for me, that not only would I be protected from danger, but that I would be true to my Lord. My! I've almost preached a sermon," he ejaculated. "Forgive me. I didn't mean to, but I had to let this out to someone and you're the victim."

"I'm glad to be the victim," Keith told him. "It's been good listening to you. I want to be your friend."

"I wondered if you really did want to be my friend," Roger said with a rather sad note in his voice. "I thought you were avoiding me. Perhaps it was because you knew what the others would be doing and you didn't want to share what was coming to me."

"I'm sorry you felt that way," Keith replied. He felt guilty, however, even though he had been avoiding Roger for another reason.

Though Faith's letters came regularly, she made no

mention of Mark, but Keith knew that she must be going with him occasionally and he tried not to be jealous.

Roger was wise enough not to witness to Keith or to try to persuade him to accept Christ as his Saviour. He felt that the Lord would lead him to do that when the proper time came. Keith was indifferent to spiritual matters and Roger didn't want to destroy their friendship, for it would prevent him from ever winning him. But he prayed for Keith constantly.

Keith was taken suddenly ill. They had been out on a hike and a sudden downpour had overtaken them. Several of the squad had colds as a result, but Keith was desperately ill for several days. When he saw the grave face of the doctor, he knew that he might have to face death. The thought of eternity filled him with terror, for he knew that he wasn't ready to face it. Roger came to see him often and he told Keith that he had been praying for his recovery. Keith smiled feebly and thanked him, but he didn't have the courage to ask Roger to pray for his soul. Through long night hours while the fever raged, he thought of Roger and wished with all his heart that he had Roger's faith and calmness and courage.

When at last he was up and about again and was able to write to Faith, he forgot his fear. She chided him for not writing sooner and he had to confess that he had been ill again, though he didn't tell her how ill he had been.

One evening when they were alone in their quarters, Roger took out his Testament and opened it to the fourteenth chapter of John.

"Isn't this a beautiful thing to remember?" he asked and began to read aloud. " 'Let not your heart be troubled. Ye believe in God, believe also in me. In my Father's house are many mansions. If it were not so, I would have told you. I go to prepare a place for you and if I go away, I will come again and receive you unto myself, that where I am, there you may be also.'

"I wonder if you thought about that passage when you were so ill?" he asked.

"I've never read that passage, so of course I never

thought of it," Keith replied, hoping that Roger wouldn't continue the subject. He had never read it himself, but he had heard it read and it didn't mean anything to him.

"I thought of it then," Roger told him quietly, "for I knew that you were not ready to meet God. I knew that there was no place prepared for you in heaven, for you had never become a follower of the Builder."

"Then I suppose I'll just be left out in the cold," Keith replied flippantly.

"No, fellow, not out in the cold, but in a place which you'll wish it was cold."

"Meaning hell, I suppose," Keith retorted.

"Yes, Keith, that's what I do mean," Roger said slowly. "I believe in a literal hell, just as God's Word says. Please don't be angry with me, but I've got to say what I've been wanting to say ever since I knew you. Have you realized that if you had died when you were so near death and when your doctor thought you would die, where you would be today?"

"In the hell you believe in, I suppose," Keith replied.

"And I would have forever reproached myself for not trying to win you for the Lord. I've wanted to talk to you about Him so often, but I didn't want to drive you away from me, for then I would have lost my chance to win you for the Lord. But now is the time, Keith, my friend, and I'm not going to let it pass. I know your mother prayed for you, for you told me so once. I wanted to talk to you then, but I was afraid it wasn't the time. Why don't you surrender now? You know you've been fighting this call for a long, long time. Now is the time to give up and yield your life to the Lord. Why not let me pray with you now?"

"There are problems that I can't face if I do that," Keith said, though he was fighting a losing battle against the urge within him to do what Roger asked him to do.

"But the Lord can settle that problem and all problems, if you'll turn them over to Him. He's done that for me so many times."

"But this is a girl," Keith admitted reluctantly. "If I do

70

what you ask, I may lose her. She's Jewish.''

He told Roger the rest of the problem.

"Had you rather lose her or lose your soul?'' Roger asked. "Don't you know that if you accept the Lord's salvation, He can take care of even that? If she is the one you should have, you'll get her, but if she isn't, He'll supply you with someone who can make you far happier than she ever could.''

"He'll have to show me that,'' Keith remarked with a weak laugh.

"He can do that, if you'll just give Him the chance in your life,'' Roger insisted. "I promise you on His Word that He can do that. How about it, Keith? I'm not saying this to frighten you or to urge you beyond your own inclination, but there is no guarantee that you'll ever have another chance to receive salvation. We never know from day to day where we'll be or what will happen. The Bible says that 'Now is the accepted time. Now is the day of salvation.' ''

As Keith looked into Roger's earnest eyes and saw the light of love and concern in them, and as the memory came to him of those very words that his mother had so often quoted to him, the wall of indifference and rebellion suddenly crumbled and he cried out, "Help me, Roger! I'll do anything you say.''

They knelt and Roger prayed, then Keith poured out his confession and asked for forgiveness. When they rose from their knees, there were tears in the eyes of both and they were not ashamed. They put their arms around each other and they clung together for a long moment.

"Thank You, Lord,'' Roger murmured as they withdrew from each other's embrace at the sound of the call for the evening meal.

"Hey! Look who's coming!'' called one of the men as the two entered with their beaming faces. "The preacher and someone who's found a pot of gold at the end of the rainbow, judging by his looks.''

"You're right,'' Keith answered with a wave of his hand. "I've found more than a pot. I've found something

71

that's worth more than all the gold in the world, for I've found the Owner of all that gold.''

''Lead me to him!'' called one of the others.

Their laughter was silenced as they stood for the short word of thanks offered by the chaplain at the head of the long table.

It was not long after this that Keith wrote to Faith the letter that aroused her curiosity about the wonderful news he had for her.

12

After the first flush of joy over his salvation had waned, Keith began to worry about Faith and the problem that confronted him. If he told her what had happened to him and as he had hinted in that letter of the wonderful secret he had, if she knew that he was really a believer and not just a nominal Christian, what would she or her mother decide about their marriage?

He knew that her mother hoped that she would finally decide to accept the Jewish faith. He had had evidence of that in the past, but he had not worried about it then, for he felt that he could convince Mrs. Marshall that he would not try to hinder Faith in anything she might want to do as far as religion was concerned. Now, however, since he had accepted Christ as his Saviour, and when he began to read his Bible and see some of the truths there that he had not even known were there, he began to wonder and to be disturbed. Finally he went to Roger and asked him about it, for it disturbed him more as the time drew near for his leave.

"I told you there was a girl back home," he began.

"I remember," Roger replied. "That was one of the

reasons you hesitated about accepting Christ. But I'm sure you're not sorry you did."

"No, I'm not," Keith told him. "I suppose you've noticed that the fellows have stopped all of their razzing. They tried it out on me just like they did on you, after that first evening when I gave them that reply when we entered the mess hall."

"What happened to make them stop so suddenly and completely?" Roger asked, for he had wondered about it.

"I had a little talk with Sam Boyd," Keith admitted. "I told him that he was the ring leader of the crowd and that I didn't mind what they said to me, but that if they started on you again, I'd give him a little lesson in judo. He had seen me giving an exhibition in that art when I first came here."

"That wasn't exactly turning the other cheek," Roger remarked as they both laughed, "but it did work and perhaps it was best to let others know that though a Christian can be longsuffering, he is not a coward."

"I think it was noble of me, for I wasn't trying to defend myself, but a friend," Keith remarked with an amused smile.

"Quite noble of you," Roger answered in the same jesting vein.

"Now about that girl," Keith said. "I think I told you that she was part Jewish and her mother hopes that she'll marry some Jewish boy. As long as I didn't care anything about religion, it didn't matter to me what she believed, because I was such a heathen that I didn't have any definite belief myself. But now it's different. I'll have to tell her what's happened to me."

"I don't think you could keep from telling her," Roger remarked. "Even if you didn't, she'd notice that something has happened to you."

"I suppose she would," Keith replied gravely. "I know I'm a different person on the inside, so perhaps it shows on the outside."

"It does," Roger told him. "And I rejoice over it. You've grown so much in such a short time."

"I've been reading my Bible as my mother hoped I

would when she gave it to me, and I've prayed that I would make up for lost time as I read it and try to understand it. But there's one thing that I read that gives me a lot of thought and a lot of worry. I'm really in a jam. That's why I came to you with the hope that you can help me.''

"What was that?" Roger asked, while he prayed that the Lord would give him the right answers.

"It was that passage in Second Corinthians that says, 'Be ye not unequally yoked together with unbelievers, for what fellowship hath righteousness with unrighteousness? And what communion hath light with darkness?' That set me to thinking. Does that mean that I shouldn't marry the girl I love if she doesn't believe like I do?''

"I'm afraid that's what it does mean," Roger answered slowly, weighing his words carefully. "You see, in Paul's day the Christians were in daily contact with either heathen — or else with Jews who didn't believe in the Lord Jesus. Paul knew that it would not only hurt the faith or possibly the testimony of believers, but that it would cause confusion in the family. We see that today in so many homes where there is division because of this very thing.''

"But suppose I would hope to win her to the Lord? Couldn't I do that?''

"If you can't win her before you're married, do you think that you would have more influence over her afterward?''

"I don't know," Keith replied dismally. "I'm just afraid that she'll do what her mother wants — and she'll do everything in her power to keep her from marrying me. But I can't give her up. I just can't. I love her more than I do my own life.''

"More than the Lord who died for you?" Roger asked earnestly.

"I just don't know," Keith replied dejectedly.

"Let's do this, Keith," Roger suggested, for he knew that he could do nothing by talking further or arguing. "Let's both pray about it. I can promise you one thing on the strength of God's Word, that if this girl is the one God wants

75

you to have, you will win her for the Lord before you marry her, or else you will find the one God has for you. Just try to pray and believe God's Word and trust Him to lead you to do the right thing. Above all, I shall pray that, no matter what happens when you get your leave, you will not deny your Lord or fail Him.''

"I'll try to do that," Keith agreed, but he wasn't too happy about the situation.

As the time drew nearer for his leave, he was still not at rest about his problem but he prayed that he would be in the will of the Lord and he prayed that the Lord would give him the courage to do the right thing and to be true to Him.

While Keith was praying and struggling with his problem, Faith was having a problem of her own. Mark was becoming more persistent in his effort to win her. When he continued to beg her to go with him to the synagogue, she went occasionally, but there was nothing in the service or the message that made her want to accept his way of life. She could never accept his faith, either to please him or her mother, for there was Keith, and she wanted to do what he would want. Though she knew that he was practically nothing as far as religion was concerned, she wasn't too sure how he would feel if she really accepted the Jewish faith just to please her mother.

She had another problem about Mark. What would she do when Keith came home? She would have to drop Mark and if she did that, then after Keith left, if she hurt Mark, he might drop her and she would be left with no one. She worried over the situation, but as the time drew near, she knew that she would be with Keith every moment possible, no matter what Mark might do or think.

Her father asked her to go to church with him again. He knew that she had been going occasionally with Mark and he wanted to try once more to help her decide the right way, whether it was with her mother or with him. He had been doing much thinking during the time that had passed since that other visit and he was not at rest about his own spiritual condition. Though they went together and he still did not hear

76

anything from the sermon that helped him, he knew that there was something in the Christian life as it had been lived by his mother and he was worried because he had not lived up to what she professed and the way she had lived. He knew that her faith was real and that it was something that he needed but which he did not possess.

On the way home, Faith turned to him and said, "Daddy, please, I wish that you and Mom would stop trying to pull me one way and then another. I wish that both of you would let me alone to decide for myself if I want to be Jew or Gentile. I was happy before and I'm all mixed up now. Just let me be like I was before Mark started begging me to go with him to the synagogue. I'm not going back there again and I don't want you and Mom to be unhappy about me. Please, Daddy, let me alone."

"I'll do that, baby," he agreed, but a sigh accompanied the words. "I suppose your mother and I are both wrong. I wonder if we were not wrong from the beginning in spite of the love we had for each other."

"Don't feel that way, Daddy. You're both happy together and I want to be happy, too. Let's just live our lives and forget our problems."

"That isn't easy to do, honey," he said regretfully.

He wondered if they could ever be as happy as they had been before this problem became such an issue between them. What would the future have for all of them? The prospect just now wasn't bright at all, for deep within him he knew that someday each of them would have to answer for the way they had lived. What kind of an account would he have to give to the God who had created him? A sigh escaped him, so deep that it seemed to Faith like a groan. Watching him, she felt her heart ache for him.

Keith's coming was the one bright spot in a future that seemed suddenly robbed of its sunshine. How she wished that he were here now, so that she could be held in his arms and be able to unburden her heart to his sympathetic ears.

13

Keith was anxious to tell Faith about his salvation and he wondered how it would affect his relationship with her. He was nervous and worried about it. He put it in the hands of the Lord and tried not to worry about it, but when he remembered Faith's mother, he couldn't help but wonder what would happen.

When Thanksgiving drew near, Faith knew that she would have to prepare Mark for Keith's coming.

Mark was disappointed when she had refused to go with him to any other services at the synagogue. Until now she had been willing to go, and he wondered what had changed her. She told him that she wanted time to think things over and he had to accept her excuse. But he wondered if she were really telling him the real reason. He knew that it would do no good to argue or plead with her and he was afraid that if he did that, she might become angry and refuse to go at all.

Mark's mother was glad that Faith refused to go with Mark and she thought that this would be a good time to try to get Mark to become interested in some other girl. She planned a surprise party for him on his birthday. In the group she invited was a young girl whom Mark had been dating before he started dating Faith.

The party was a dismal failure as far as her plans were concerned. When the guests had all arrived and Mark saw that Faith wasn't in the number, he drew his mother aside and asked why she was not invited.

"Because she's not really one of us," she explained "and she would have felt out of place in this group."

He said nothing, but he was as uncongenial as he could be without being actually rude and his mother was disappointed and angry over her failure. She rebuked him about the way he had acted when the guests had left.

"You were terrible," she told him. "You didn't even try to be polite to Jane when she sat alone over there hoping that you would ask her for a dance. You stood there watching the others as if you didn't see her at all. I'm glad that Herbert was polite enough to ask her."

"I didn't want to see her," he told her. "Mother, you might just as well give up the hope of making me fall in love with one of those girls, because I don't care for them and I never will. I love Faith and if I can't have her, I don't want anybody."

Finally Faith knew that she would have to tell Mark that Keith was coming. The opportunity came when he was taking her for a ride.

"Keith will be coming home for Thanksgiving," she said. "He'll be here for only a little while and I'll have to be nice to him. I hope you won't be angry if I can't be with you while he's here. Please don't mind."

"I will mind and I'll try not to be jealous, but I'll be glad when he's gone again. You like him a lot, don't you?"

"Yes, I do. We've been friends for such a long time, ever since we were children," she confessed.

"That doesn't make me any happier," he remarked morosely.

"You shouldn't feel that way," she told him. "Can't I be friends with both of you? You've been with me so often while he's been away, so it's only fair for me to be with him during the short time he'll be here."

"He's in love with you," he stated. "Even a blind

person would've known that.''

''That doesn't mean that I can't be friends with him and with you, too,'' she argued. ''Didn't I tell you that I wasn't ready to be tied down to anyone for a long time yet?''

He was silent and she felt like a hypocrite, but she didn't want to make Mark angry, for she knew that when Keith left, she would still need him.

Keith came home a day ahead of time. He was sitting in the porch swing when she came home after a date with Mark, as he had done before he went away. It was a warm night for that time of the season and he was enjoying the peace and quiet of the lovely night while waiting for Faith. Her mother had told him that she had gone for a ride with Mark and he suspected that she was glad to give him that information.

He was jealous, as he had always been, but he tried to overcome that feeling as he waited for her.

When Mark stopped the car and helped her out he went with her to the door. Before he told her good night, he begged her for just one kiss.

''It'll be the last time I'll get to see you again until that guy leaves,'' he pleaded. ''Please, just this once.''

Faith didn't know why it was that she refused him, but she did so.

''No, Mark, and please don't ask me. I'm tired, so please tell me good night and let me go inside.''

''When may I see you again?'' he asked, disappointed.

''I don't know. Please go. Good night and thanks for a pleasant evening,'' and she turned to the door while Mark ran down the steps and got into his car, then drove away at racing speed.

As she started to open the door, she saw Keith sitting there and she uttered a little cry.

''Don't waken the neighbors, or you'll have the police coming for me,'' he warned.

''Keith!'' she cried excitedly and ran into his outstretched arms. ''I didn't expect you until tomorrow.''

He kissed her long and clingingly, then held her close.

"What a fright you gave me!" he said when there was time for speech. "I was afraid I'd have to sit here and watch that fellow kiss you. If he had, I'm afraid there would have been a battle. I suppose it was Mark. I believe that's what you called him."

"Yes, it was," she admitted, meanwhile thanking whatever providence she believed in that she hadn't let him kiss her.

"I can see that he's been trying to take you away from me while I wasn't here to defend my rights," he said, with pretended severity.

"You know he never could do that. You're in my heart forever and forever. He's been nice to me and it's helped to make the time less lonely while I've been longing for you every hour of every day."

"That's a very pretty speech, but just how much of it can I believe?" he asked playfully as he held her.

"Every word of it. You know that I'm telling the truth, cross my heart and hope to die."

They rocked to and fro while she rested in his arms with her head upon his shoulder.

"It's heavenly to have you home again," she murmured happily. "I shall begrudge every hour that passes, because I know that in such a short time you'll be leaving me again. How can I stand it, with another year and three months to go before you come home for good?"

"It will pass sooner than you think, with such a good friend to make you forget your loneliness," he reminded her.

"That isn't a bit nice," she rebuked him. "Please, let's talk about us. Tell me everything that has happened to you and what you did and everything."

"I think I've pretty well covered that in my letters," he replied.

"Have you told your mother about us?" he asked presently. "I was hoping you would."

"I told you that I couldn't tell her," she reminded him. "I promised her and I broke my promise, so I couldn't tell her the truth. She's been happy because I was going with Mark, so I just let her be happy. I did tell Dad that I loved you and I think he was glad.''

"So you kept your ring in its box," he said regretfully. "I would be so proud to see you wear it."

"I'll wear it now," she told him. "I won't hold out any longer, because it's so beautiful and I've been longing to wear it."

"How about Mark? Won't that give him a shock? Then you'll be left without any admirer while I'm gone again.''

"I've made up my mind," she stated. "It won't matter what Mark thinks, because I can wait and be lonely, if necessary."

"If I'm not shipped overseas before my next leave in the spring, I want us to get married. Would you be willing to have just a quiet wedding and then go with me to the west coast and live near the base until my time is over?''

"Would I!" she cried. "You know I would. I'd be happy to go with you anywhere. When will you be coming back?''

"Perhaps soon after Christmas. I split my leave so that I could come back in the spring. Since I've come at this time, it's only fair to let some of the others be home for Christmas, for some of them have wives and children. Would you like that?''

"Anything you say will make me happy, as long as you don't stop loving me," she told him.

"That will never be," he replied as his lips sought hers.

"You said you had something wonderful to tell me and I've been so anxious to know what it is. What is it?" she asked, suddenly remembering.

The exuberance of his joy suddenly vanished and a cloud hung over his happiness. He had forgotten his problem in this time of reunion.

"Let's let that wait until another time," he advised. "Tonight, let's just talk about our wedding and our life together after that.''

As they talked, with Faith doing most of the talking, for he was thinking and was somewhat depressed, he wondered if there would be any wedding. Would she fail to yield to his pleas to accept the salvation which he possessed? Would he have the strength to hold out in obedience to the command of the Lord? Or would he fail that command and run the risk of disobedience instead?

14

Keith knew that his time was short and that if he was to be able to marry Faith and at the same time not disobey his Lord, he would have to get about witnessing to her with the hope and prayer that she would accept his Saviour before he had to leave.

He came the next afternoon and they went for a ride.

"Now I want to know what that wonderful news is," Faith insisted as soon as they were on their way.

"You might not think it's so wonderful when you hear it," he began, trying to choose his words carefully and looking to the Lord for guidance. "It's such a simple thing, but it means everything to me and I'm hoping that you will be able to go along with me in sharing it."

"What is it?" she asked impatiently.

"It's just this," he said slowly. "I've accepted the Lord Jesus Christ as my personal Saviour."

She looked at him with wide eyes. She was aghast and disappointed. He uttered a silent prayer for guidance.

"What do you mean by that?" she finally asked.

"I mean that I came to realize what I surely knew all along, that I was a sinner and that I was a lost soul because I had failed to ask God to forgive my sin and to save my soul. A buddy of mine made me realize what a dangerous position I was in and he made me realize how rebellious I had been by refusing to do what I felt all along that I should do. I got on my knees and I asked the Lord to forgive me and to save my soul for the sake of Jesus Christ who shed His blood for my sins on Calvary. He did that very thing and I've been a different person ever since. I've not only had peace in my heart, but I realize that others have seen a change in me. I can't describe that change, but I know that when a person is different on the inside, there is bound to be a change on the outside.''

She was silent and he could see the disappointment on her face.

''Is that all?'' she asked. ''I thought you had some wonderful plan for us because of something great that had happened to you.''

''But something great has happened to me and I do have a wonderful plan for us,'' he insisted. ''I want our life together to be as perfect as a marriage could possibly be. But the only way that can be is for both of us to believe the same thing as far as our spiritual life is concerned. We both know how unhappy life can be when there is disunity in the faith of two people who are supposed to be one in marriage. You can see it in your family, that even though your parents love each other, they are unhappy and disturbed because of what their marriage cost and about your lack of religious belief.''

''Do you mean that you expect me to believe that Jesus of Nazareth is the Son of God and my Messiah?'' she asked, much perturbed.

''I'm hoping and praying that I can convince you that He is,'' he confessed. ''If you could only read your Old Testament Scriptures with an open mind, you would be convinced that He is. Every prediction concerning His birth and death mentioned in the Old Testament has been confirmed in the New Testament by His birth, life, and death and by history.''

"That's what your people say, not mine," she retorted bitterly.

All the joy had faded, leaving bitterness and disappointment that followed in the wake of his avowal. She was thinking of her parents and how their perfect happiness had been marred by this same difference, even though her father confessed to nothing and was only living upon a memory of what his parents had been.

"But if your people would only read their Scriptures with an open mind and not have their vision blurred by all the addition of man-made laws in the Torah, instead of taking the unadulterated Word of God as your own people wrote it, they would believe just as I do. Please let me try to explain and make you see that what I believe is the only way for you to have eternal life."

"And not go to hell, as your minister said in those two sermons I heard him preach," she said bitterly. "He was condemning everyone who didn't belong to his denomination, to that hell. Mark says that a true orthodox Jew doesn't believe that there is a hell. The writers of his faith say that there is no hell, that the word is only found in the New Testament and, of course, we don't believe that."

"But your father does," he insisted," and if you'd tell him what I've been trying to tell you, he would say that I was right."

"My father doesn't believe in anything, even though he is a Gentile, so his opinion doesn't count with me," she replied coldly. "If you hope to make me believe in your Christ, you're wasting your time, because I refuse to depart from my mother's faith. After all, she is more loyal to her belief than my father is and I choose to follow her."

"I see that Mark has been doing all he can to help her win you to that faith," he remarked. "I suppose he has taken you to the synagogue," he added as he began to feel utterly inadequate.

"I've tried to be fair," she told him. "I went with him and I went with my father, but I didn't receive any more enlightenment from that preacher than I did from the rabbi.

They both clouded the issue for me. I suppose I'll just continue to be a heathen,'' she finished on a bitter note.

"But I don't want you to continue to be a heathen," he said tenderly as he stopped the car upon a shaded stretch and put his arm around her. "Faith, my darling, if I could only explain what has happened to me since I believed and had my sins forgiven. I've received a new nature along with the old and I've received the gift of eternal life. And there is a peace in my heart that I never had before. Always there was the gnawing conviction that I wasn't living right, even though my morals were above reproach. I knew that God was speaking to my heart, yet I refused to listen to His voice. Now there is such joy, even though sometimes I may not be happy, that I want you to have that same peace and joy. Then our life together would be perfect. Won't you try to see it and let the Lord come into your heart as He came into mine? Then you'd know from your own experience what I'm trying to explain."

She withdrew from his arms and replied coldly, "I don't see why I should. I'm happy and satisfied to remain just as I am. You'll have to take me just as I am, or else."

"That's the thing that's hurting me," he said, trying to draw her to him, but she refused to let him. "I can't take you as you are. If we're to be married and live happily together, you'll have to give your life to the Lord just as I did. Then together we can be yielded to His will and there will be a little heaven on earth. And if there are any children, there will be no question or secret battle between us as to how they shall be instructed in spiritual matters."

"Do you mean that if I don't accept your Christ and believe that He died for my sins, you won't marry me?" she asked.

"I mean that I can't and still be true to the Lord who saved me," he replied slowly and sadly. "You see, He says in His Word not to be unequally yoked together with unbelievers. He knows what unhappiness such a union will be. There can be no real and lasting joy outside of Him."

"You're more narrow-minded than either my mother or father," she remarked bitterly.

"But neither of your parents have been really true to their beliefs," he argued. "For that reason, you shouldn't be so determined not to believe what I believe. It's not narrowness, it's just obeying God as an obedient child should obey a parent who loves him."

"Then if I don't believe what you believe, I'll not be good enough to marry you," she stated.

"I don't mean that at all," he denied, gaining possession of her again and holding her close. "I still say that I love you more than I do my own life, but another, greater love has come into my heart, the love of the Christ who shed His blood for my redemption and who loved me enough to die for me so that I might not have to have the experience of eternal death. It isn't a question of your not being good enough, but a question of obeying God or refusing to obey Him. The one leads to happiness in His perfect will and the other will lead to disaster. Please try to look at it the way I do and let me try to show you why Jesus Christ can be your Saviour. Just as He became mine. It is so simple, yet so wonderful, this miracle of salvation. I'd give my life right now, just to know that He had won your soul and that you trusted Him as your Saviour."

She withdrew from his arms again and there were tears in her eyes.

"Take me home," she said. "I don't want to hear anything more."

"Please don't make me do that," he begged. "I'll promise not to mention this any more, but just hope that you will think about it and I'll pray that God will open your heart to the truth. Don't let's lose this whole afternoon. I have such a short time to be with you."

"I want to go home," she insisted. "The afternoon is spoiled. I want to be alone."

He said nothing more, but turned the car around and drove slowly home with her. His heart was heavy. He had prayed so earnestly that she would believe and that, somehow, God would perform the miracle for which he was hoping.

They said practically nothing on the ride back and when they reached her home, he looked at her long and earnestly. He couldn't kiss her there on the street in the daylight, though he longed to.

"May I come tonight and take you out to dinner?" he asked with pleading in his eyes and in his voice.

"I don't know," she answered. "I have to have time to think. If I'm not good enough for you, why do you still want to be with me?"

"Because I love you so much, with every breath and every heartbeat, and because I'll never have another happy moment if you refused to love me."

"Where would that joy be that you talked about so glibly a while ago?" she asked sarcastically.

"It would still be there. It will always be there, no matter if I should have my heart broken. It's a joy that the world nor anything in the world can give, not even you, for neither the world nor you can take it away. It's something that's greater than even my love for you. But even if you never let me see you again, I'll love you with my last breath. I shall be praying that God will enable you to understand this wonderful experience that I've had and that He will enable you to have the desire to share it with me. May I come tonight?" he repeated.

"Phone me and I'll let you know," she told him.

She went into the house without a backward glance or a parting smile.

He drove away with a heavy heart, but with the persistent prayer that her soul would be saved, no matter what the cost might be to him.

How fortunate that a merciful God conceals the future and that He does it in love.

15

Faith's mother knew that something was wrong when Faith came in and hurried to her room. She hoped that Faith and Keith had had a quarrel, but she decided not to ask questions. When Faith didn't come down to dinner she went to her room and knocked on the door. When she went in, she saw Faith sitting beside the window and she could see that Faith had been crying.

"Dinner is ready, dear," she said. "We're waiting for you."

"I don't want anything, Mother," Faith told her. "I have a bad headache. You and Daddy go ahead without me."

"Why not lie down and let me bring something to you later on?" her mother suggested, but Faith told her that she didn't want anything.

After her mother had left, she sat there and looked dismally out the window through tear-drenched eyes. So utterly miserable was she that she couldn't think straight. She tried not to think, for thinking brought memory of what had happened and caused the tears to flow again. The future looked hopeless.

Keith couldn't, or wouldn't marry her unless she

changed her whole way of thinking and accepted his way — and that seemed impossible. Yet she loved him so much that she would be willing to do anything just to belong to him. But how could she do what he asked when that seemed such an impossibility?

The more she thought and the more she tried not to think, the more miserable and confused she became. She decided that she had better go to bed and try to sleep, even though it was so early. She went to her closet to get her gown, when her mother knocked at the door again.

"I'm going out to see Mrs. Barnes," she said. "Your father will be here, if you want anything."

"I'll be all right, Mom," Faith assured her.

Soon after her mother had left, her father came to the door.

She was glad that he had come, for she wanted to talk to someone and he was the only one to whom she could look for comfort. She knew that she couldn't talk to her mother about her problem.

"How are you, dear?" he asked as he came in and sat down beside her.

"I feel terrible, Daddy," she told him. "I'm glad you came, because I want to talk to you."

"It's about Keith, isn't it?" he asked.

She nodded, for she couldn't speak. She was on the verge of tears again.

"I suspected as much when your mother told me you had been crying. It's heartache, not headache, isn't it? Have you two had a quarrel?"

"It's something worse than a quarrel," and tears flooded her eyes.

"Tell me about it," he urged.

"You remember that I broke my promise to Mom when I told her that I wouldn't let anything be decided between us when Keith went away. He asked me to marry him and he gave me a ring, but I couldn't wear it because I didn't want to hurt Mom by letting her know that I had broken my promise."

"So you played around with Mark to keep her from suspecting," he said reproachfully. "That wasn't fair, honey."

"I was trying to do what Mom wanted, so I went with Mark to the synagogue. I went, not only to please her, but to see if I could accept her faith. And I went with you so that I could be fair to both of you, but I couldn't accept either faith. I didn't see anything in either of them that would help me spiritually. However, I did believe like Mom believed, that Jesus of Nazareth is not the Son of God and not our Messiah.

"Now Keith has been, what he calls, converted, and he says that because his Bible says that believers shouldn't marry unbelievers, he can't marry me. That makes me feel that he thinks he's better than I am. This has broken my heart," and her voice quivered.

"Is that the way he put it?" her father asked.

"No. He put it in a much kinder way. He begged me to believe what he believed and he quoted that passage in his Bible word for word. He said he'd give his life if I could just believe what he believes, for there is such peace in his heart since he has believed."

"I know just what he means," her father said with a heavy sigh.

He was remembering what his mother had quoted to him before he married. But then, he wasn't a believer. Now he knew he had disobeyed what he knew to be true when she had told him that there would always be a division between them because of the difference in religious belief.

"What can I do, Daddy?" Faith asked in a voice choked by sobs. "I love him and I want to belong to him. If I don't, then my life will be ruined. I don't think I could ever be happy again."

"Then do what he asks," her father advised. There was pain in his eyes and upon his face.

"But how can I?" she asked after a moment's surprised silence. "How can I believe that Jesus is the Son of God when He isn't?"

92

"Why are you so sure that He isn't?" her father asked.

"Because Mom has taught me that He is only an imposter, a good man, perhaps, but not the Son of God and not our Messiah."

"Your mother has broken her promise to me," he said regretfully. "She promised not to try to indoctrinate you or influence you until you were old enough to make your own decision. So you needn't feel too bad about not keeping faith with her."

"I think she did that after you began taking me to Sunday school," Faith told him. "She wanted me to have both teachings. What can I do, Daddy? Please help me. I can't go on like this."

"I repeat, try to believe what Keith tells you about Jesus Christ, that He is the Son of God. I wish that I had the same faith that he has and that I had had the same strength in that faith that he has. Perhaps all of our lives would have been different and much happier. It's true, what he told you, that there can be no real happiness and peace in a family when there is not the same faith about spiritual matters."

"I thought that you and Mom loved each other so much that you were happy in spite of this difference," she said.

"We do love each other, and in a measure we have been happy, but there has always been the memory of the sorrow we caused the ones we loved by our marriage, for the same reason you're now facing. Then there has always been our uneasiness about you, though we have seldom spoken about it. You have grown up with no belief at all, only your determination not to believe that Jesus is the Son of God. Since Keith has such decided faith, a faith which I knew about from your grandmother, my advice to you is that you try to believe the thing he believes. I realize what a wrong I have done by not accepting the faith of my mother. It has gnawed at my heart many times and it still does that, tonight stronger than ever."

"What will Mom say? I don't want to hurt her."

"Your soul is more important than your mother's hurt feelings," he said decisively. "What Keith was trying to

93

make you believe was what I heard all my life. Yet I turned my back upon it because of my love for your mother. What he told you is true, even though you don't believe it. Jesus is the Son of God and He died on a cross for your sin and mine, as well as for the sin of the whole world. When you believe that, you'll understand what Keith tried to make you believe and what I'm telling you. Just listen to him, honey, and be happy. That's what I want for you above everything in life.''

"I'll try, Daddy,'' she promised as he kissed her good night and left her.

Keith hadn't called and she was disappointed, but she thought that it was best that he hadn't. She was in no mood to talk to him.

Keith had decided that he wouldn't call her. He would wait and let her decide if she wanted to see him again. He prayed about it and he counted on the Lord to answer his prayer in His way and in His time.

The next morning Faith called him and told him that she was sorry she had been so cross the day before and that he could come whenever he wanted to. He came that afternoon and they went for a ride and for dinner afterward.

Faith told him that she'd had a talk with her father and that he wanted her to try to accept Keith's faith.

"I'll try, Keith, but I don't have much hope that I shall succeed,'' she warned.

"We'll leave that to God,'' he replied.

"Tell me more about what happened to you and how it all came about,'' she requested.

"It was after I had been ill. I didn't tell you how sick I was, but I was pretty low and my buddy, Roger Mills, had a talk with me after I recovered. He made me see what a dangerous position I had been in, that if I had died, I wouldn't have been ready for eternity, but would have been a lost soul through all that eternity. And, Faith, eternity never ends.''

"But the Jewish belief is that in eternity we grow better and become fit to live with God through the ages,'' she argued. "And, like I said, they don't believe in hell.''

"My darling, if you're going to try to believe what I

94

believe, you're going to have to believe the whole Bible, that it is the Word of God, handed down by the Holy Spirit through men, and that there are no mistakes in it. And the Bible says that we are either saved or lost souls. We're born with a sinful nature and with physical life, but there is no spiritual life until we come to God and ask for forgiveness and for salvation. Then He forgives us and we have eternal life and are born again.''

"I'm going to have to undo all of my thinking to accept that," she said, "but I shall try, for I want to do what you want me to and I want to be what you want me to be — and to believe what you believe."

He took her in his arms when he had stopped the car beside the road and murmured, "It's not what I want you to believe, my darling, but what God wants you to believe, for He loves you so much that He sent His Son to this earth to shed His blood on Calvary for your sins as well as for mine."

"I'm afraid it's going to take a long time for me to believe," she said regretfully, "and the time is so short. We can't make any plans to get married if I can't say that I believe. I can't make any plans on an uncertainty and I know you wouldn't want to either."

"I shall pray that it won't be as long as you fear. Will you go to church with me Sunday?"

"I'll go, but if what I hear isn't any better than what I heard when I went with Dad, it won't help much."

"This church is different," he told her. "I believe you'll hear something there that will help you, for I know the preacher. I went there a few times, but my mind was closed to the truth. It's the church my mother attends. When we go there, I'll be praying that you'll hear just the right words and that you will open your heart to them. How about it?"

"We'll see what happens," she replied.

When they parted, Keith's hopes were high, but Faith was still wondering what would happen. She was willing to do what Keith wanted her to do, but his explanation of what had happened to him left her with no desire to believe. Not that she didn't want to, but she just didn't. She felt indifferent to the whole plan of salvation. Her heart had been hardened and her spiritual sight had been blinded by the teaching in the years which were most impressionable. As she had told Keith, she would have to undo all that she had been taught to believe.

16

Faith told her mother that she was going to church with Keith. Her mother was determined not to worry over this situation, for she knew that Keith would be leaving soon and that perhaps after he was gone, Mark would renew his attentions and that this might do what she hoped for.

The church they attended was quite different from the one she had attended with her father. It was small and there was nothing ornate in the interior, though it was neat and attractive. There was a piano at the front and young girl was playing as they entered.

There was little formality when the service began, the singing of a few hymns and a prayer, after which the offering was received, then another prayer and the preacher began his message. If Faith had had any previous training in the Word and its application, perhaps she would have been interested, but since she did not, she began to let her mind wander while the preacher continued his message. When he had finished, before the last hymn was announced, he urged everyone to return for the evening service, for it was then that the visiting evangelist was to begin his week's service.

Keith didn't ask her what she thought of the message

and Faith didn't enlighten him. He was satisfied that she had been willing to go with him and hoped that before the meetings were over, she would have given her heart to the Lord. That was what he was praying for.

He didn't ask her to go with him to the service that night, for he thought that the beginning service would be more of a setting up for the services to follow and he didn't want her to feel that he was pressing her. However, when he asked her to go with him on Tuesday night, she objected.

"Do we have to go to that meeting every night?" she asked. "There is so little time left for us to be together."

"But there is so little time left for you to hear the plan of salvation so that you can really believe," he argued. "The service won't last long and we can be together afterward. It will make me happy if you'll go."

She agreed to go night after night and they went until the last one on Friday night. Faith tried to listen, but she found it impossible to believe what she heard, for she understood so little of what the preacher took for granted that his audience would know. If he had been able to deal with her personally and to show her from the Bible just what she needed to know, perhaps she would have understood and believed, but as the meetings drew to a close and she didn't seem any more convinced or convicted, Keith was terribly disappointed. On the last afternoon of the meetings, he spent a long time on his knees, praying that God would work the miracle and that she would accept Christ as her Saviour.

Faith listened attentively to the message, for she knew that this was the last night of the meetings and her last chance to believe. She had no more desire to accept salvation than she had at the beginning. The veil which Paul spoke of concerning her people, was still on her heart, keeping her from seeing the truth clearly.

Keith felt desperate. He had asked her the night before, if she wouldn't try to believe and yield her life to the Lord, but her reply added to his disappointment.

"I need time, Keith," she said. "Please give me a little more time."

"But there is no more time," he told her in desperation. "The meetings are coming to a close and I'll be going away in a few days. I can't leave you like this. I want this thing to be settled before I leave, for if it isn't then where will our plans be for a wedding? I'll never have a happy moment, if you don't accept the Lord."

"I'll try," she promised. "I have tried," but she wondered if she ever would.

When the sermon was finished on that final night, Keith waited tensely as the minister gave the final invitation for those who wanted to receive Christ as their Saviour, to come forward and kneel at the altar. He had been praying all during the message that Faith would go forward, for he knew that if she didn't there was nothing that he could do if the minister had failed.

When others began to go forward until the altar was almost filled, and Faith made no move to go, he finally turned to her and whispered, "Darling, won't you please go, if only to make me happy?"

She hesitated a moment, then without answering, she rose and took her place with the others at the altar.

Perhaps, even then, if someone had come to her and talked to her from their experience in dealing with souls, the result might have been different, but even so, God had His plan through it all, though the ones most concerned couldn't see into the future and know what that plan was.

While she knelt there wondering what was coming next, with no desire within her heart except to please Keith, a young girl knelt beside her and whispered, "Now that you have come forward and signified that you want to be saved, just pray through and God will hear you and save your soul. I'm so glad that you came."

She placed her hand upon Faith's head as if she had been a little child, then left her. Faith was as unenlightened as when she first knelt there. How could she know how to pray through, she asked herself, when she had never really prayed and didn't know how? She was as cold and unyielding as she had been before the message and the meetings began. She still had her doubts about Jesus of Nazareth being the Son of God.

Finally, after a short prayer by the preacher, for those who had come forward, that the step they had taken this night might lead them to grow in the knowledge and the joy of their salvation, they all arose from their knees and the meeting was dismissed.

Loved ones and friends came forward and crowded about the altar, and embraced those who had knelt there. There were tears of rejoicing. Faith stood alone, wondering what she should do, until Keith came to her and led her toward the door with his arm around her.

"My darling, I'm so happy that at last you've done the thing for which I've been praying," he whispered as they paused a moment outside in the darkness.

He took her in his arms and kissed her and she clung to him while the tears came. She didn't know why she was crying, but she knew deep within her that nothing had happened to change her. But she couldn't let him know the truth. She'd just have to let him keep on being happy. He would be gone in a few days and she wouldn't have to tell him.

"All I want is to make you happy," she said as they got into his car and drove out toward a little restaurant not far away.

"You've made me the happiest person in the world," he said. "Now that you're saved, there's nothing to prevent us from being married when I come back in the spring. Will you be my wife then, Miss Marshall?" he asked.

"I shall be honored, sir," she said in the same playful tone, but her heart was heavy.

She was wondering what would happen if he should find out before they were married, that she wasn't really a believer, that she hadn't accepted Christ as her Saviour.

She wouldn't think about it now. She had so little time to be with him and she was determined not to let perplexing thoughts spoil the few remaining hours of their happiness together.

As they ate a light lunch, they discussed plans for their

wedding. They agreed that, for the sake of Faith's mother, they would be married quietly, with just a few friends present. They both knew how her mother would feel and they wanted to do as little as possible to add to her unhappiness.

While they talked, Faith tried to forget the worry that gnawed at her and marred her perfect joy at the prospect of belonging to Keith. When he kissed her and left her, murmuring again how he thanked the Lord for bringing her to Him, she felt like a criminal as she responded to his caress.

She decided that if she didn't feel any different before they were married, she would try to feel different afterward and she hoped that, if this didn't happen even after that, then he might not find out the truth. She didn't realize that it wouldn't take Keith long to discover that she was not really a believer, that she was not born again. He would know that if she really loved the Lord, that she would reveal it, not only in her response to his remarks, but in her daily life. It would reveal itself in her unconscious attitude toward spiritual things.

The next day when Keith came for her, she was wearing his ring. He noticed it the moment he met her.

"I'm glad to see you wearing that," he remarked. "Since you're no longer ashamed to wear it, I suppose I'd better have a talk with your father and see if he's willing to let me take his daughter off his hands."

"I'm sure he'll be glad to be rid of me," she assured him. "I don't know how Mother will take the news, but she'll just have to get used to it. I wish I could keep from hurting her, but there is no way to do that."

Keith had his talk with Faith's father that very night. Mr. Marshall did not hesitate to tell Keith how glad he was when Keith asked for his blessing.

"You've got it, my boy," he replied. "I couldn't wish for anything better for her than to have you for a husband. I'm sure you'll make her happy. God bless you both," he added with a smile.

When Keith had joined Faith, Harry Marshall sat there thinking and the smile faded from his lips. He was thinking of the time he had asked for his wife's hand. It had been a terrible experience, so different from what had just passed between Keith and himself. That father had been so bitter. He remembered the heartache of himself and the girl he loved, to know what their love was costing those who loved them.

Though they had been married both by a minister and then by a rabbi, it made no difference in the father's bitter and unforgiving heart.

He was determined that nothing like this should happen to Faith. He knew how his wife would feel, but he would remind her of their promise to each other and he would do his best to make her sorrow lighter.

When he told his wife that night, he was not surprised at her reaction.

"You've won!" she cried. "You've won! But I'll never be happy again, if she marries that boy."

"You shouldn't say that," he urged. "Just remember what we've suffered and remember how our hearts have been grieved. Please don't do to Faith what your people did to us. Try to accept what we can't help. You had your chance with her and I did nothing to interfere when I knew that Mark was doing everything in his power to convert her to your religion. Let's do all we can to make her happy. After all, isn't her happiness more important than our own? It isn't a matter of who has won. Just try to be happy with me for a little while longer."

He held out his arms and she came into them while she wept silently. Presently she raised her head and kissed him lightly upon his cheek.

"You're right," she said while the tears still rolled down her cheek. "Her happiness is more important than either yours or mine. I'll try to be reconciled and pray that God will forgive me for not bringing her up as I should have."

"And I shall pray, something that I haven't done for a long time," he said sadly, "that she will be happy and that you will be glad that you kept your promise to let her be happy in her own way."

Faith was wondering how she would manage to keep Keith from knowing the truth. She promised herself that she would read the little New Testament he had given her and that she would try to be what he wanted her to be. She felt like a hypocrite and she knew she would be acting a lie, but, without knowing how to ask God for enlightenment or help she made her resolve in her own strength to so live that he would never find out the truth until she perhaps really lived the truth — after they were married.

17

Faith tried to share Keith's happiness as they made plans for their wedding, but her joy was tempered by the knowledge that she was living a lie before him. She made a determined effort not to let this interfere with the joy of being with him during the remainder of his time with her.

He was at the house most of the time, for, now that he was to be a member of the family, he was welcome to be there. Faith's mother showed Keith every courtesy, even though she wasn't happy over the situation.

They took long rides in the afternoon and after dinner in the evening. Keith's mother had Faith over to dinner and she told Faith how glad she was that she had accepted Christ as her Saviour. Faith responded, hoping that she was saying the right thing and feeling terribly guilty.

One evening as the two drove along off the highway and out of traffic, Keith remarked, ''I hope that you understand what salvation means, now that you're saved. You will be able to understand your Bible better and it will be more precious as you read it, for the Holy Spirit will give you a much better understanding. The Bible says that the natural man, that is, the person who's not saved, can't understand spiritual truths, for they are foolishness to him. I wonder if you're beginning to find that out."

"Not completely," she said, "but I shall keep on trying to understand. It's been such a short time since I went down to the altar. I'm sure I shall, in time."

"I'm sure you will," he replied. "I'll let you know where I'm reading and we can keep up with each other. That way, you'll seem nearer to me than ever while I'm away."

"That will be wonderful," she said, but there was no enthusiasm in her heart.

When the time of parting came, after Keith had told her parents good-by, he and Faith were alone. Faith couldn't keep back the tears. He wiped them away gently and kissed her tear-wet eyelids, then her full red lips.

"Don't do that," he remonstrated. "It makes me want to cry, too, and I don't want to be a baby. Just remember that every moment I'll be away from you, I'll be praying for you, that you may be kept safe from harm and that you'll grow in the joy of your salvation."

She burst into sobs that she couldn't control while he held her and waited for the sobs to cease. Little did he suspect the cause of those sobs.

"How can I grow when you're not here to teach me?" she finally managed to ask. She was afraid that he might suspect the truth as conscience stabbed her.

"Just trust the Lord and read His Word and pray for guidance," he advised. "And remember that it won't be many weeks until I return for you. Then we'll be together and we won't ever have to be parted for long. Remember that and dry those tears. I'll be living for the day when I can return. We'll count the days together."

When it was time for him to leave to board the midnight plane, she clung to him as if she couldn't let him go. He gently released her and kissed her tenderly for the last time and then left her with a smile and a kiss that he blew to her as he closed the door.

When she went to her room and began to undress, she

removed Keith's ring and held it for a moment while her tears again fell upon it. She felt that she had no right to wear it and she knew that while Keith was away, every day would be filled with the fear that somehow he would discover the truth of her deception.

The days passed monotonously for a while after he had left, for not even Mark phoned her. Finally, when she felt that she couldn't stand the loneliness any longer, Mark phoned. He asked her if she would be willing to go out with him, now that Keith had gone. She was so relieved to have the opportunity to get out of the house that she told him she would be glad to go with him.

When she dressed for the date, she hesitated as she took the ring out of its box. She didn't know whether to wear it or not. If Mark saw it, he wouldn't want to continue dating her, but she wanted to wear it, even though she really had no right to. She used that as an excuse and put the ring back into its box and closed the drawer.

She had a pleasant evening with Mark, though at times she was bored by his conversation. She couldn't keep her thoughts from Keith and she compared him to Mark. Mark let her know that he still hoped to win her, if she was not already promised to Keith.

"I know that you do care for him," he told her, "but I'm not going to give up hope that you'll learn to care for me. If old Keith finds someone else and lets you down, I'll still be here to comfort you and love you."

"That's not a very comforting thought," she told him. "You're not very flattering to either Keith or me."

"I know it," he acknowledged, "but I want you to know where I stand. I'll be willing to just wait and hope and be with you as often as you'll let me. I'm not making any pretenses and I hope you won't make any either. Be honest with me, Faith. If you can't give me any hope, tell me so. But let me see you, no matter what. That's all I ask."

"Then I will be honest with you," she said. "Keith and I do have an understanding. If he doesn't go overseas, he'll be back here in the spring and we'll be married then. He gave me a ring, but I didn't wear it tonight because I didn't want to hurt you.''

His face was grave and he didn't say anything for a moment, but presently he said, ''I was afraid of that. But what I said still stands. Just let me come around occasionally and I'll try to be satisfied with your friendship, if that is all you can give me.''

She was touched by the sadness in his voice.

''I like you so very much, Mark,'' she told him. ''And I do want your friendship. If you still want to go with me, knowing the truth, I'll be grateful, for I'll be very lonely.''

''I'll be glad for that, at least,'' he said dolefully.

After that, she decided to wear her ring. She felt ashamed of herself for not wearing it in the first place. Mark made no mention of it when they were together again, but she saw him looking at it and she felt sorry for him. She knew how she would feel if the situation were reversed.

Christmas came and Keith sent her a present which disappointed her. It was a beautifully bound Bible with notes and footnotes. On the flyleaf under her name was a chapter and verse number from the Song of Solomon. He purposely omitted the words, for he wanted her to look it up. She spent quite a while looking for it, but when she found it and read it, tears came to her eyes. The passage read, ''Set me as a seal upon thy heart, as a seal upon thine arm, for love is strong as death.'' He had run a pencil mark through the rest of the verse that read, ''jealousy is cruel as the grave — ''

He had written to her almost every day since they had parted, but soon after the first of the year she stopped hearing from him. She was afraid that he might be ill again. Then she received a letter saying that he might come sooner than he had expected. She waited a few days, eagerly expecting that surprise, but he neither came nor did he write.

One morning the paper bore the headlines that a plane had gone down in waters that North Vietnam claimed to be within their boundary. All on board had been lost. The names of those lost had been telegraphed to the nearest relatives and now the list was made public.

They were at breakfast and, as usual, Faith's father was reading the headlines while waiting for the hot cereal to be brought in. He uttered an exclamation and he clutched the paper as he read further, then he put the paper aside, while he glanced at Faith with such horror in his eyes that she exclaimed, "What's the matter, Daddy? Have those Vietnamese killed some more of our men?"

"Let's not talk about it until after breakfast," he said as he strove to keep the horror out of his voice.

Just then the cereal was served and he made a pretense of eating. Some terrible premonition took possession of Faith and she got up and picked up the paper. When she saw Keith's name among those lost, she dropped the paper and stood there with white face and stricken eyes.

"It can't be! It can't be!" she cried in broken tones. "It can't be!"

Her father rose and went to her to try to give her some word of comfort, but she turned and fled to her room. She threw herself upon the bed while sobs shook her and she pounded her fist upon the pillow as she lay there wracked with torture. Presently her mother came in and tried to talk to her, but she motioned her away and didn't answer her. She couldn't, for she was weeping too violently. Her father came later, but had no better success.

She lay there during the rest of the day, crying at times, moaning when the tears stopped for a while, then lying there inert with utter exhaustion. Time had suddenly ceased. She was adrift upon a sea of darkness, being borne along by torture, bitterness and despair.

The next day it was the same. Her mother came again and tried to rouse her from what seemed like a coma but Faith turned her head away and motioned to her to leave.

Finally that afternoon when Mr. Marshall came home and they discussed the situation, they decided to send for the family physician. He advised them to leave Faith alone, that she would be better if they wouldn't try to make her talk. He left a prescription for a sedative if they thought she would take it and then, after assuring them of his sympathy, he left.

He knew that no medical help could heal the wound that Faith had received. What none of them realized was, that there was only One who could give peace and strength to go on in a time like this and, since none of them really knew that One, there was no one else to give real and lasting strength and peace. Only time would tell what the result would be.

18

When Faith came down to breakfast on the second morning, she looked so pale and broken that her parents worried. She kissed her mother dutifully before she sat down and her father came and kissed her before he sat down. They began the meal in silence, for no one knew how to begin the conversation. They wanted to say something that would comfort her, but they were afraid that they might say the wrong thing. They had no comfort to give her.

Finally Faith spoke. "Why don't you say something? Don't be afraid to talk. I can take it."

"We'd like to be able to say something that would help you to understand how our hearts ache for you," her father began, "but I know there is nothing that can help at a time like this. Time alone can heal your hurt. You know that we love you and all we want is to see you happy."

"Time won't help, Daddy, and I know I never expect to be happy again," she said in a dull, hopeless voice. "I've got to live with it, but I just don't want to live. Let's not talk about it, because talking about it only makes it worse."

They obeyed and tried to talk of other things, little items

her father had seen in the paper, while Faith toyed with her food and sat there silently and brooding.

The next day was Saturday and her father was at home. He asked her if she wouldn't like to go with him on a little business trip to the next town, but she refused, saying that she had a headache. While he was away, her mother heard her walking back and forth in her room and she longed to go to her and try to comfort her, but she knew that she had no comfort to give her.

In the afternoon Faith's friend Amy phoned her and asked if she might come over and see her, but Faith told her that she wasn't feeling well enough to talk. She had passed the stage of crying, but she sat by the window and looked out on a world that had lost its beauty. She saw nothing but a future without hope or happiness, a future where memory would always be there to bring agony that would never diminish, no matter what might come to her.

She wished that she could take her life, but she didn't have the courage. What lay beyond this life might be even more terrible than the one she would have to face in the future. If there was a hell, she would without a doubt enter it, if what Keith believed was true. So her thoughts continued to whirl round and round in circles and they brought no comfort, only confusion and despair.

That evening when her father returned and found her sitting drearily in the living room, he sat down beside her and put his arm around her. He began to tell her about his visit and of the near accident that had occurred on his way home.

"I stopped my car and thanked God for saving me," he remarked. "Just a few inches more and that car would have knocked me clean over that embankment to a horrible death. I want to go to church tomorrow and thank Him again in the proper way for saving me. How about going to church with me, honey?"

"I don't want to go to church, not ever!" she exclaimed vehemently.

"I thought you would love to go since you went with Keith," he said. "God still loves you, dear, and perhaps it

111

would be a comfort to you if you would go. I'll take you to the church where you and Keith went.''

''God doesn't love me!'' she cried in bitter tones. ''And I don't want anything to do with Him! If He loves me, why did He take Keith from me, just when we were going to be so happy together?''

''Don't talk that way, Faith,'' he warned. ''It's dangerous. I thought you had changed.''

''I wanted to believe, but now I don't,'' she replied. ''I just don't want anything to do with church or religion or anything that pertains to it. It's all a form and a sham. There's nothing real in it.''

''Do you think that what Keith had was a sham?'' he asked in grieved tones. He was thinking how he had failed this child of his because he had failed God himself.

''I don't want to talk about it, Daddy. Please don't talk about it any more. I can't stand it.''

She rose and went to her room. He sat there thinking and as he did, he remembered how narrowly he had come to having his life snuffed out. He shuddered as he realized that if that had happened, he would now be in eternity without Christ, a lost soul because he had failed to listen to his mother's pleas and to the voice of the Holy Spirit who had beckoned to him so often — to yield his life to the God who loved him and the Saviour who had died for him. If he had done that, then perhaps his whole life would have been different. He might have won his wife, for she would have seen something in his life that she didn't have. And his child might now have the one Comforter whom she needed and for whom she held such bitterness.

When morning came, he went to the church that Keith and Faith had attended and what he heard that morning smote his heart with such conviction of his sin that he asked the Lord to forgive him and to save his poor sinful and neglected soul. When he returned home, he had a peace in his heart that he had never known before. When he thought of all the wasted years, he wondered how God could forgive him for such waste. It was almost more than he could do to keep from telling what had happened to him, but he knew that this wasn't the time, so he prayed that he would choose the right time and that his testimony wouldn't be wasted.

When time had passed and Faith was able to resume a more normal attitude, her father told her what had happened to him. She listened apathetically and told him that she was glad for him if he could believe, but that there was no use to try to make her believe, for there was nothing in her heart to make her want to believe. He knew that there was still bitterness and resentment, that she did not think of her unworthiness to receive God's blessing, but only of the sorrow for which she blamed Him.

One afternoon Mark called and asked her if he might take her for dinner and a ride afterward. He told her that he knew how she must feel and that he gave her all his sympathy.

"I thought you might like a little time away from home," he explained. "I promise not to bore you with any conversation, but just to take you for a little outing. You don't have to talk at all if you don't feel like it. Please say you'll go."

She couldn't tell him how glad she was of the opportunity to get out of the house and to be away from torturing thoughts for even a little while, but she did tell him that she would go with him.

Her mother's hopes revived when she saw them leave, for, now that Keith was out of the way, perhaps Mark's persistence would win after all.

"It was thoughtful of you to ask me," Faith remarked as they drove along.

"It was kind of you to go with me," he replied. "I know that I can't say anything that would help you to bear your grief, but at least I can let you be sure that I'm your friend and that I want to do everything that I can to help you to be happy again."

"Thank you, Mark. I can never forget and I don't feel that I'll ever be happy again, but I do know that time will make the pain less and that I'll be better able to bear it. And I do thank you for being so considerate. I want you for my friend.''

He did his best to keep her mind off herself and she did her utmost to respond to his efforts and before the evening was over, he saw her smile again. It gave him encouragement. When he left her, she promised to go with him again soon. He still had the hope of winning her and he determined not to give up trying.

As time passed, he became a frequent visitor at the house and had dinner with them often. Faith began to look upon him as someone upon whom she could lean in her sorrow and as time continued to pass, the keenness of that grief became less until she could laugh at his little jokes and she realized that she enjoyed being with him.

Mark began to hope that she was falling in love with him. When he told her once that she was the only girl he had ever loved, she didn't rebuff him, but let him continue what he was afraid to say.

"I still love you, Faith, more than ever," he told her. "I know that you could never love me as you loved Keith, but won't you give me some hope that you'll let me do all in my power to make you happy? If you'll only give me the chance, I promise that I'll try. You can't go on living like this. Someday you're sure to fall in love with someone, even though you have Keith's image enshrined in your heart — so please let that someone be me.''

"I'll promise," she conceded.

"Thank you," he murmured. "I'll live in hope but I won't annoy you. I'll wait until you're ready to give me a chance. I'll just be longing for that time to come sooner than you think.''

Why not give him the chance to try to make her happy? she asked herself. He was kind and thoughtful. He loved her and she could depend upon that love to take care of her and to keep her from being so miserably lonely. She could never love him as she had loved Keith. She felt that she could never really love again. Love seemed to have died with Keith, but she could try, and in the presence of his love she might find a

114

shadow of what happiness would have been if Keith had lived.

Mark continued to be devoted, though he never pressed her for an answer to his love. Finally one evening when they were driving after dinner, she turned to him with a smile.

"You once asked me to marry you, remember?" she asked.

"How could I forget!" he exclaimed, wondering what was coming and hoping.

"You said you would wait for my answer. Are you still waiting?"

"I'll keep on waiting and hoping as long as I live," he stated.

"I'll marry you, if you really want me," she said with a little smile.

"If I want you!" he cried. "I want you more than anything in the world."

They had reached her home and when he had parked the car he held out his arms and whispered, "Please."

She let him hold her and he bent down and kissed her. His lips were warm and tender, but hers were cold and unresponsive. If he noticed, he made no comment. He realized that her heart still remembered Keith, but he was satisfied. He would make her love him as much as he loved her! That would be the purpose of his life from now on.

When Faith reached her room, she looked out into the darkness as she heard him speed away. She wondered if she had done the right thing, if, even as his wife, she would be content with life, or if she would still go on in her suffering and the longing for someone who would never return.

Presently she turned away and began to undress. What difference did it make what she did, marry him or not? Nothing would ever be the same and she might as well make him happy as to sit alone and brood. She would at least have his love and companionship and after all, nothing would ever matter too much to her anyway.

19

The next morning when Faith made the announcement of her promise to marry Mark, the news was received with different emotions. Her mother was delighted and made no secret of her joy. It was what she had hoped for for so long and now that hope was realized.

Her father said nothing and Faith didn't ask him what he thought, for she already knew. When they were alone while her mother was in the kitchen, he called to her as she was leaving the room.

"Wait a minute. I want to talk to you," he said, leading her back into the living room. He pulled her down beside him on the couch and put his arm around her. "My little one, are you doing the right thing by marrying Mark?" he asked tenderly. "Are you sure that you can give him the love that he should have from a wife?"

"I'm sure that I'll never love anyone in the same way that I loved Keith," she replied as her voice wavered for a moment. "Mark loves me and I like him very much. If I can make him happy, perhaps a little of his happiness may rub off on me, but I doubt that, for I never hope to be happy again."

"But you will be, if you'll just give yourself time. I

know how terribly your heart aches now, but I know that time will take some of the ache away and in time you may meet someone you can really love and not just like. That kind of emotion won't make you happy and in time Mark will begin to resent your lack of real love and there will be unhappiness and discord. Do take my advice, Faith, and wait and don't rush into this marriage hastily. Give yourself more time."

"I don't believe time will help," she stated stubbornly. "He loves me and he's been so kind even when he knew there was no chance for him. I don't want to disobey your request, Daddy, but I believe that I'll be better off if I marry him than I would be, just sitting around here and thinking of what might have been. I'll have someone who will try to make me forget and even if I can't do that, I'll at least not be so terribly unhappy. I've given my promise and I feel that I should keep it. Please don't be angry with me, Daddy."

She laid her head upon his breast and a little sob shook her.

He bent down and kissed the top of her head.

"I'm not angry, dear, just worried. Do you realize that he will want you to be married in his faith and that you will have to become a true Jew if you expect happiness either with him or with his mother?"

"I've thought of that, but it doesn't make any difference how I'm married. Since I don't have any belief of my own, I might just as well follow his religion if it will please him. I'll be no worse off than I am now."

"But since I've accepted Jesus Christ as my Saviour," her father said, "I know that it will make a big difference. You'll be turning your back on the Lord you wanted to know when Keith was here. Then you'll be in a dangerous position. Please think of that. I want to see you believe as I do, as I've been praying that you would. I've been praying that your mother would also come to believe in the Lord Jesus, who is really her Messiah."

"It would take a miracle for that to happen," she said as she raised her head and withdrew from his arms.

He let her go, but he sat there looking after her as she

went upstairs. His heart was heavy. If he had been the kind of father he should have been, this wouldn't be happening. If she married that young Jewish boy and tacitly accepted his faith, she would be more lost than ever from the hope he had of winning her for Christ. Her mind would be darkened and the veil would be there, hiding the truth from her. He sighed heavily as he got up and prepared to leave for his place of business.

When Mark told his mother that Faith had promised to marry him, she was terribly disappointed. She still hoped that he would fall in love with someone who was firmly fixed in his own faith. Now what would happen? She was already beginning to dislike Faith.

When she asked Mark how they would be married, he said that he had not asked her about that. He was just happy that she was willing to marry him.

A few evenings later he asked Faith about that. "I want you to marry me as soon as you can," he began. "Won't you set a date, so that we can begin to make plans?"

"What's the hurry?" she asked. "Aren't you satisfied that I'm willing to marry you?"

"Of course I am, but what's the use of waiting? I've waited so long that I'm tired of waiting. Why can't we make plans now?"

"There won't be the need of many plans," she told him. "I don't want a big wedding. I want it to be a quiet one with just the family and close friends. I don't want any invitations sent out."

"I would like to have a few of Mother's friends. It would please her."

"She can invite them personally," she told him. "If invitations are sent out to her friends, then my friends would feel neglected and I don't want that to happen."

"You act as if you're ashamed of marrying me," he said.

"You know that's not the reason, but don't you understand? It's been such a short time since — since — and I don't want to be the subject of a lot of gossip. People would

118

think that I had forgotten mighty soon. I'd feel embarrassed, with a lot of people there who're not real close friends and would probably not understand.''

"Would you be willing to be married by our rabbi?'' he asied. "It would make my mother much happier.''

"It doesn't make any difference who marries us. Whoever you want, only just let it be sort of private.''

"You act as if you're being taken to your execution instead of a wedding,'' he said bitterly. "If you don't love me, Faith, I don't want you to marry me. If you do that, then we'll both be unhappy. I want you more than anything in the world, but I don't want you without your love.''

"I'm sorry, Mark,'' she said contritely. "I didn't mean to act like that. I do love you as much as I'll ever love anyone, but I want to be honest with you. I don't love you like I loved Keith, but I know I can never love anyone like that again. If you're willing to take the love I can give you, I'll try to be a good wife and to make you happy.''

He took her in his arms and kissed her tenderly. She tried to respond to his kiss, but there was no warmth in her heart, no glad fluttering as her lips met his, just the yielding to their possessive pressure.

"I'll take whatever you can give me,'' he whispered, "and I'll try to be satisfied with that. Just try to love me as much as I love you. If you can't, then I'll accept what you can give me.''

"You're sweet,'' she said and caressed his cheek. "I'll try with all my might and main,'' and she smiled a mirthless smile. There was the memory of other arms that had held her and of other lips to which she had responded with all the warmth of her being.

The wedding was set for a few weeks away, for Faith had yielded to his request for an early marriage. Her mother insisted upon buying an elaborate trousseau, so that she wouldn't be ashamed when she became a member of Mark's family. Faith had shown so little interest in the purchase of the dresses that her mother couldn't fail to notice, but she said nothing. She knew that Faith was still thinking of Keith and that she was not too enthusiastic about this marriage, but she hoped that in time she would forget the pain and be happy with Mark.

She and her husband talked the matter over, but they decided not to interfere in any way. Though Faith's father was more perturbed as the day drew nearer, he said nothing. He had said all that he could. He decided that all he could do was to pray and try to have faith that all would be well.

The two families met together and became better acquainted. When Mark's mother learned that Faith was willing to be married by the rabbi, she was in a better frame of mind. She liked Faith's mother and she decided that they would be a congenial family.

Mark was living in the clouds and counting the days until Faith would belong to him.

As time passed, Faith became more uneasy. She was thinking more often than ever of Keith and that if he had lived they would have been married and together in a dream world of their own. She remembered what a thrill it had been to buy the needed things for her trousseau and how she dreamed as she selected the pattern for her wedding dress that was to be made by a French seamstress.

Now there was no wedding dress to be made. One was to be bought from one of the bridal shops. Faith had put that off until the last minute. She just couldn't go down with her mother and try on a wedding dress. If she did that, the thought of what might have been would be more than she could take and she would burst into tears. She didn't want that to happen. Finally her mother spoke to her about it.

"You ought to go down with me tomorrow," she said, "and look at the dresses. They may not have one your size and if there were too many alterations, it might take longer than we have time for. You should have let Madame Fleury make it as you had planned before."

"Not tomorrow," Faith objected. "I'll be going out with Mark and we'll probably be home late. Let's wait until Monday."

Her mother reluctantly agreed. She was worried because Faith seemed so reluctant and so indifferent about buying what should be the most important dress of her entire life. If she could have known what was in Faith's thoughts, she would have been more worried.

The thought of trying on that wedding dress seemed more than Faith could stand. She spent the time until Mark came for her in an agony of indecision. By the time he came, she had reached a decision. She was pale and nervous all through lunch and her parents noticed it.

"What's the matter, honey?" her father asked as she sat there silent and ate so little. "You look as if you were going to your execution."

"Perhaps I am," she said gravely. "Not my own, but perhaps that of someone else."

"Do say!" he remarked jovially, trying to make her smile. "Just whom do you plan to kill today?"

"No one, I hope," she said with an attempt to smile. "I'm sorry if I look so glum. I'll try to do better."

"That's much better," he said as she gave him a brighter smile. "I don't want my daughter to go to the altar looking like a ghost."

She didn't reply, but the smile faded as thoughts came that she couldn't put into words. If she went to that altar, there would be a ghost of a memory and a dream that could never be realized — the ghost of someone who should have been waiting for her at the end of that aisle, instead of the living presence of the one who would be there, the one to whom she would belong for the rest of her life.

20

When Mark came for her and they drove away, she noticed that he seemed excited about something. His eyes were shining and his voice exhibited suppressed excitement. She wondered what it was, but she didn't ask, for she had her problem and it wasn't pleasant. She wondered how she would be able to tell him what she felt she must. Her courage slipped away as they drove on while he kept up a flow of conversation.

Finally they came to the little restaurant where they usually dined and they ordered their meal. She wondered when he was going to tell her what was on his mind, as he continued to ramble on with small talk.

When they had finished their meal and had taken their places in his car, he didn't start the car. It was quite dark outside and they were in a secluded spot with only the lights from the restaurant showing dimly through the darkness.

"I've been waiting so impatiently for this moment," he told her. "I've something I want to show you. I hope you'll like it."

He took out a little box and opened it. She uttered a

surprised gasp as she saw what the box contained. It was a beautifully set diamond, larger and even more beautiful than the one that Keith had given her.

"I wanted you to have it right away," he said, "but I had a hard time getting your size. Now won't you please take that other ring off and wear this one?"

He took the ring out and held it, waiting for her to remove the other ring, but she made no move to take it off her finger.

"I know you prize that ring a lot, but it isn't fair for you to keep on wearing it," he said as she still made no move to remove the ring. "I know you'll want to keep that ring and I won't mind, but you're engaged to me now and Keith is just a precious memory."

She spoke slowly and with difficulty, for she knew how her words would hurt him, but she had to say them just the same.

"Oh Mark! I'm so sorry you did this!" she cried in a voice that shook in spite of her effort to control it. "I can't take this ring off. I expect to wear it always. I was going to tell you tonight what has been weighing so heavily on my heart that I couldn't put it off any longer." She waited a moment until she gained courage to continue. "Mark, I hate to have to tell you this, but I just can't marry you. I just can't!" Her voice broke and a sob choked her.

"You can't marry me!" he exclaimed. "I don't believe you. What's come over you, Faith?"

"It hasn't just come over me," she managed to say, her voice quivering as she strove to hold back the tears. "It's been building up within me ever since I promised to marry you. Every day that brought our wedding nearer, I began to rebel against the feeling that possessed me, that I tried to overcome, but I wouldn't be overcome. I hated to have to tell you and I kept putting it off because I knew how it would hurt you. I know now that I can't go through with it. It wouldn't be fair to you. You'd know that I didn't love you and you would be disappointed and hurt and you would grow bitter and our marriage would be a failure. It's better not to be married than for that to happen. Now you'll be free to find someone who will really love you and you'll be happy with her."

He sat there silent for a while, then he put the ring slowly back in its box. He turned to her and his voice was accusing.

"Why did you lie to me and make me believe that you loved me? Why did you promise to marry me if you felt this way?" he demanded.

"I thought I could love you, Mark. I thought I could make you happy. I did try to make myself believe that I loved you, even though I told you the truth, that I could never love anyone in the same way that I loved Keith. Now I know that I still love him so much that I can't love anyone else. I just can't. I'm sorry."

"Sorry!" he ejaculated. "You should have been sorry enough not to lead me on in this fool's paradise. You've done a cruel and unforgivable thing!"

"I'm sorry, Mark. That's all I can say," she said humbly. "Please forgive me. I did what I thought was the right thing to do, but I know now that it would be the worst thing I could do, if I married you, knowing that I couldn't love you."

"It's a pity you didn't find that out sooner," he exclaimed bitterly, "before I bought this ring."

"You can take it back," she replied.

"That will make me look like some kind of a fool," he said in that same bitter voice. "What will everyone say when they find out that you've thrown me over?"

"They don't have to know the truth right away," she suggested. "We can tell them that we decided not to get married just now. In time, when they learn that there isn't going to be any wedding, their curiosity will have been forgotten."

"That won't satisfy my mother," he retorted. "She'll know what a fool you've made of me."

"I have an idea that she'll be glad you're not going to marry me," she said. "I don't think she approved of me."

"She didn't, at first, but when you consented to be married by our rabbi, she was satisfied. And all the time you knew you'd never be married to me! No wonder you were so willing to let me have my way about it."

"That isn't true. I went ahead with my plans for the wedding. I bought everything for my trousseau, but as the time drew near, I just felt I couldn't go through with it. Then I would indeed be leading you on with a lie. You should thank me for telling you now instead of letting you find out later when it would be too late."

"Just forget the whole rotten mess!" he cried as he started the car and turned out on the highway.

She didn't answer while he drove so fast and so recklessly that she was afraid he would wreck the car. In his present mood, she didn't know what he might do. She was glad when they reached her home.

He didn't get out and help her out as he had always done so gallantly, but let her get out while he sat behind the wheel.

"Good night, Mark," she said as she stood beside the open door. "I'm sorry you're so angry, but, believe me, I did what I thought was best."

"Good night," he said and reached over and shut the door before she turned away.

She was surprised at his rudeness. She had never witnessed this side of his disposition before and a little sigh of relief escaped her while she felt that a great weight had been lifted from her. Life would not be all sunshine with such a disposition. When things went wrong and his feelings were ruffled, she could imagine what his reactions would be.

How different it would have been with Keith! He wasn't perfect, but she had seen him under stress and anger and he had never been like this. She realized what a blow this had been to Mark and she felt sorry for him, but she was glad to be free again from the weight of dread and repugnance that had burdened her.

The next day she told her parents what had happened. She wanted to wait until they had finished their meal and were sitting in the living room together. She came in and sat beside her father while he finished reading the paper, then he turned to her with a smile.

"Where's lover boy, little one? It doesn't seem natural to have you sitting here with us like this."

"He won't be coming here anymore," she told him gravely.

"Why, what's happened?" her mother asked in alarm. "Have you two had a quarrel?"

"I told him that I couldn't marry him," Faith replied quietly.

"Why, I can't believe you, Faith! What made you do a thing like that?"

"I did it because I knew I couldn't marry him. I knew that I didn't love him in the way I should and I knew that if I married him there would be no peace in my heart and that before long there would be none in his — and there would be a broken marriage. I thought it would be more kind to him to let him know now than to wait until after we were married. I knew that I could never go through with it."

Her father uttered a sigh of relief. He had felt all along that Faith was making a mistake, but he had said all he could and he knew she had made up her mind and that he couldn't change it.

"I think you've done the right thing, honey" he told her. "You did the right thing by telling him now before an unhappy marriage took place."

"Thank you, Daddy," she said.

"How can you say that?" his wife exclaimed. "What a blow it must have been to Mark! And what will people say when they know that the wedding is off and such a short time to let people know?"

"I think Faith's happiness means more to us that Mark's or what people may say or think," her husband said gravely. "Don't you want what is best for Faith?"

"I thought this marriage was best and so did she," his wife retorted. "I can't imagine what changed her mind."

"Nothing but my own feelings, Mother," Faith told

her. "The nearer the time came, the more I knew I couldn't go through with it. I had to tell Mark just how I felt."

"Poor fellow!" her mother exclaimed. "I know his heart is broken."

"He was pretty angry with me," Faith informed her. "He didn't act very politely either."

"You can't blame him, no matter how he acted," her mother argued.

"I don't blame him. I blame myself for thinking that anyone could ever take Keith's place."

"You won't always feel that way, little one," her father asserted, putting his arm around her. "Just give yourself time and the right man will come along and you'll be happy again with him."

"The right one has already come and gone and I never expect to be happy again," Faith said in muffled tones as she buried her face on her father's shoulder and cried softly.

21

Faith's mother was so disappointed and so angry with Faith that she made life miserable for her. She didn't speak to Faith except when she had to and when she did, it was in a cold, disapproving voice that cut Faith and hurt her deeply. It added to her unhappiness at a time when she needed her mother's comfort and help the most.

"Why do you treat me as if I'd committed some crime?" she asked in desperation when this had been going on for several days and she felt that she couldn't endure it much longer.

"You've done such a terrible thing," her mother responded coldly. "I'm disappointed in you and ashamed to think that my child could do such a thing to a fine boy like Mark. What will his people think or say?"

"You're caring more of what people will think and of how Mark feels than you do of how I feel," Faith told her. "I don't care what people think or say. I'd rather have them say it now than to wait and to have them say the worst if there was a divorce — and there certainly would be one if I married Mark feeling like I do. I do think, Mother, that you might have a little more feeling and consideration for me. I need your love and your sympathy, yet all I get is silence and reproof. I can't take it much longer.''

"Then why don't you try to undo the wrong you've done and tell Mark that you'll marry him?'' her mother persisted.

"How can you suggest such a thing!'' Faith cried angrily. "In the first place, he wouldn't want me after I've told him how I feel toward him. Why can't you be reasonable? I've done what I thought was the only right thing to do and that's all I intend to do. I'm sorry if I've disappointed you, but I thought you loved me enough to try to bear your disappointment without making me feel like a criminal.''

Finally Faith went to her father. If he had noticed how his wife was acting, he didn't reveal any evidence of it. She hated to hurt him or to cause any trouble between them, but she knew that she could expect the comfort from him that she hadn't received from her mother.

"I can't take it any longer, Daddy,'' she said when she had told him how her mother had been treating her. "Mom makes me feel that she doesn't even love me any more. She's only thinking of what Mark's people will think of her and how our friends will gossip about it. I know there will be a lot of gossip and a lot of hard feelings among Mark's people, but I can't help it. I did what I thought was best and I still think so.''

"I know you did, dear. The mistake was in trying to enter a marriage when you were not sure you were in love with Mark. Remember, I warned you.''

"Please don't make it worse by reminding me,'' she begged with tears in her eyes. "I know that was wrong, but I thought I could learn to love Mark and I did want to make him happy. I wasn't thinking so much about myself, because I was so desperate that I didn't much care what happened to me. I'm sorry that I didn't listen to you.''

She buried her face in her hands and wept softly. He took her in his arms and held her while he caressed her gently.

129

"Don't cry," he murmured. "I know what a terrible time you've had and what a struggle you've had just to keep on going. Just be patient and I know your mother will snap out of this before long. If she only had the love of God in her heart, she wouldn't act like this."

"I can't sit by and wait for her to change, Daddy, I just can't," Faith sobbed. "I can't endure it any longer, or I'll crack up. I want to get away somewhere, anywhere, just so I won't have to listen to the gossip and questions that the girls will soon be asking and to endure Mom's bitterness. I've got to get away, Daddy. Where can I go?"

"I'll think of something," he told her. "Just give me a few days and I'm sure I'll find a way out of this and perhaps when you return, you'll have a different outlook on life and your mother will have time to get over her disappointment."

"I'll go anywhere you say, Daddy. Do you have any place in mind?" She was beginning to feel calmer already.

"Just you wait and see," he advised. "Just be patient for a few more days and we'll see."

She didn't press him further. She was satisfied that he would help her and it didn't matter to her where he planned for her to go, just so she got away from the home that was now so unhappy.

Mr. Marshall had read the ad of a personally conducted tour to Europe and the Holy Land before Faith had told him about what she had done. He had thought of making plans for her to go on this trip and surprise her so that she might be able to let time heal her grief. But while he was thinking about this, she had told them of her engagement to Mark and he had given up the idea.

After his talk with Faith he phoned the tour director and asked if it was too late to make a reservation. He was assured that it wasn't too late and he made application at once and sent the check on. When he had made all the necessary arrangements that could be made without Faith's cooperation, he was ready to tell her what he had done.

When his wife had left for a meeting, he called to Faith to come down. She was in her room wondering when she

130

could get away and hoping that her father would soon reveal some plan for a trip somewhere, anywhere.

When she came down, eager and hopeful, he sat down beside her and held out a little brochure of the trip he had planned for her. As she glanced over it, her eyes widened.

"You mean that I'm to go on this trip?" she asked.

He nodded. "Everything's been arranged but getting your passport and your vaccination certificate. You'll have to go down with me to get the passport and our doctor can get that vaccination taken care of. Think you'll like it?"

"Would I?" she exclaimed. "It's what I used to want more than anything, but, remember, when I asked you to let me go, you said to wait until I was old enough to really appreciate it."

"Then you became interested in other things. I'm sure that the Lord has kept this waiting for you until just the right time."

A shadow crossed her face for a moment, for she was still bitter toward the Lord and she didn't think that He would do anything for her good. He had already done the worst.

"It surely has come in just the right time," she agreed. "I can get away from it all for a while and I know that when I come back, I'll be better able to take whatever comes. Thank you, Daddy. Thank you so much. What would I do without you? How can I ever thank you enough?"

"By trying to be the kind of girl the Lord wants you to be. I shall be praying for that as long as the Lord gives me breath," he said gravely.

"I want to do anything that will please you, because you're all that I have left." Her lips quivered as she thought of her mother.

"Don't say that, dear. You still have your mother. I'm sure that she loves you. She'll soon get over her disappointment. You'll have to get ready for that trip, because you have only a little time before you'll be leaving for New York."

When Faith went to her room, she was too excited to sleep. She opened the brochure and read every word over and over again. The next few days were hectic days, but she was nearer to being happy since Keith had died. She was kept so busy that she had no time to think of what had happened or to be hurt by her mother's coldness. She was so busy that she saw very little of her mother except at meal time.

Her mother was amazed when she knew about the trip and hurt with her husband for not telling her what he was planning. He reminded her of how unkind she had been to Faith and that he thought it would be best for Faith to get away for a while until she could assume a more considerate attitude toward her. Their conversation wasn't too pleasant, for it was the nearest to a quarrel that they had ever had, but when they ended their little session, she had to admit that she had been unkind and that she was sorry.

Finally the day came when Faith was to leave on the first lap of her trip. Her father drove her to the airport. He was glad that his wife didn't want to go with them, for he wanted to have these last minutes with Faith all to himself.

"Just remember while you're away, that I'll be praying for you every day, that you will have a safe journey and that you will get the utmost out of everything that the Lord has for you," he said as he went to the gate with her while they waited for the call to board the plane.

"Thanks again for everything, Daddy. I love you and I shall be thinking of you and thanking you for every pleasant hour on the trip."

She wished that he would keep God out of it. She wanted to try not to think of Him at all.

She kissed him and he hugged her tightly for a moment. There were tears in his eyes as he watched her trim little figure walking toward the plane, climb the steps and become lost to sight as she went inside.

A little smile hovered upon his lips in spite of the moisture in his eyes. He didn't tell her that this tour was conducted by the president of a Christian university and that most likely all of the people who would be with her would be real believers. He left that for her to discover and he put it all in the hands of the Lord, for he knew that he would be praying that in some way unknown to him, but most surely known to God, she might find peace in the One who was crucified for her sin and had shed His blood in order that that sin might be forever washed away.

22

It was not until Faith was on her way across the Atlantic, flying toward Paris, that she realized that she was going on a tour with Christian people under the auspices of a Christian college. She was surprised and shocked and then she became angry, for she knew that her father had known this when he made arrangements for the trip. She knew that he had done this purposely, so that she might come to accept his belief that Jesus of Nazareth was her Messiah and the Son of God.

If she had discovered this before the plane had left the airport, she would have refused to go, but there was nothing she could do now, but make the best of this unhappy situation.

Faith had met Ethel Conrad who was to be her roommate on the trip and she had been attracted to her almost from the first. She had been asleep when Ethel had come in and undressed so silently that she didn't waken her, but the first thing the next morning Ethel introduced herself and told Faith that she was glad that they would be roommates.

She asked Faith where she lived and then she told Faith

that she was a teacher at Johnson University which was sponsoring the trip.

When they boarded the plane, she and Ethel became separated and she had to sit with two young men who were with the tour. She was sorry about this, for she had looked forward to being with Ethel, but soon the one sitting on the seat next to the aisle left to sit by his friend in the rear and she was left with the other one.

"I suppose we'd better get acquainted, since we're going to be together for quite a while," he said. "I'm Ray Crowell."

"I'm Faith Marshall," Faith told him. "I see your friend has deserted you."

"Oh, he has a girl friend he wants to be with," Ray told her. "They're already acting like an old married couple. They both attend Johnson University."

"Do you attend there?" she asked.

"No. I graduated from there two years ago. I'm pastor of a little church in Virginia. They were kind enough to give me this trip."

"Oh! Then you're a preacher!" she exclaimed and immediately she began to freeze.

"One of sorts," he said with an apologetic laugh. "I'm just getting adjusted to the work. I love it and the opportunity it gives to meet people and try to help them with their problems and to have the opportunity to lead souls to the Lord."

She felt so ill at ease with him now that she wished she could change her seat. She looked back longingly to where Ethel sat, enjoying conversation with another member of the group. Of all things! Not only to be in a Christian group, but to sit with a preacher for the next several hours. How she wished that she were back home. Anything would be better than this.

As Ray continued talking, she began to feel more at ease, for he was a good conversationalist and she was interested in spite of herself. He mentioned some intriguing facts concerning the places they would see and she became more interested, but when he mentioned the fact that there were five preachers in the party, her heart sank. What a dull time she would have on this trip!

"We'll have to watch our step with so many preachers in the party," she remarked.

"You won't have to do that any more than you would at home," he told her. "These men are out for a good time and they won't have any ministerial dignity, if that's what you're worried about. But then, you know, a real Christian doesn't have to watch his step when he's away from home any more than he would if he were at home. Isn't that true?" and his eyes became grave.

"Yes, it is," she agreed. "We can't help but reveal our real natures, no matter how we may try to conceal them, for the truth will come out before we realize it."

"How right you are," he replied.

As she uttered those words, she wondered how soon it would be before some of them would know that she was not what she pretended to be. She remembered how she had deceived Keith and how she had been afraid that he would discover that she had only pretended when she had gone down to that altar and professed to be a believer. She felt that if these people should discover the truth about her, they would ostracize her. Little did she understand the spirit of the true believer, or she would have been even more disturbed, for she would have known that the main desire of each of them would be that she would become what they were.

Before lunch was served, she and Ray were carrying on an animated conversation and laughing together at some funny remark. She had forgotten her animosity. He was quite good-looking and she confessed that, even though he was a preacher, he was interesting and she enjoyed being with him.

As they approached Paris, they both enjoyed looking out of the window at the landscape beneath them.

"I never hoped to see this place," he remarked as the plane approached the airport and began to circle for a landing. "This trip is a gift from the Lord. Everything else that I ever got was by hard work and digging for it. I worked my way through college," he said, turning to her with a smile. "It was worth it. It all led to this wonderful trip. I shall be eternally grateful for it."

"I have my father to thank for my trip," she told him. "I do hope it will be all he said it would be." She had her doubts, for her conscience was beginning to bother her.

"It will be everything that you could hope it will be," he assured her. "We'll see practically everything of interest throughout the whole trip. Of course the Holy Land tour will be the highlight for all of us. I'm sure you feel the same way."

"I know it will be wonderful," she replied, but her words sounded hollow and unconvincing in her own ears.

Why should that part of the tour be more interesting than the rest of it? She would be glad to see the land from which her mother's ancestors had come, but aside from that and the thrill of seeing new places that she never expected to see, there was no thrill of anticipation.

When the plane landed and they were ready to disembark, Ray waited for her to go out ahead of him.

"I've enjoyed these few hours together," he told her. "I hope that we'll be seeing more of each other."

"Thank you. I've enjoyed it too," and she smiled up at him.

Ethel joined her as they went toward the terminal building and started to go through customs to have their baggage examined.

"Didn't you like Ray Crowell?" she asked. "I think he's a wonderful person."

"Then you knew him?" Faith asked, surprised.

"I knew him when he graduated," Ethel told her. "He won the highest honors in his class. He's making good in a great way in the church that he pastors. I hope you like him. I would have joined you, but I saw that you two were getting acquainted and I didn't want to be a third party."

"I was a little awed when he told me that he was a preacher, but I soon found out that he was human, after all. I like him very much."

By the time they had reached their hotel and were assigned to their rooms, it was time for bed. They unpacked the few things that they would need for the night and for the next day's sightseeing, then Ethel took out her Bible and began to read as she lay in bed.

Faith wondered what Ethel would think of her because she didn't read also. She had put her Bible in her suitcase at the last moment. It was the last gift that Keith had given her and she had promised to read it, but she had never kept that promise. She decided that she would get it out the next night and read a little from it. She didn't want Ethel to discover that she was not a believer. She would have to watch her step carefully and that would keep her anxious the whole time.

When Ethel put out the light and told her good night, she tried to sleep, but conscience began to hammer at her. What a terrible hypocrite she was! What a terrible thing she had done to Keith when she had deceived him about her salvation. Then she suddenly remembered that she hadn't knelt to pray as Ethel had done just before she put out the light over her bed. Ethel would wonder, if she didn't pray. How could she pretend to do that? But she would have to, unless she wanted Ethel to discover the truth. She could pray, or she could pretend to pray. She could pray to the Lord Jehovah, even though she was bitter toward Him and though she had never prayed to Him before. She decided that she would kneel there, even if she didn't utter a word.

The next morning when the alarm went off, Ethel bounced out of bed with a cheerful good morning, then knelt by her bed in prayer before she began to dress.

Feeling like the worst kind of hypocrite and deceiver, Faith knelt also and tried to pray, but no words would come. She feared to try to talk to God when she felt so bitter toward Him. She knew that she had no access to Him, that He would not even hear her if she tried to pray. She remembered how she had spoken about Him to her father and fear increased as she knelt there in silence. Shame possessed her and as she rose from her knees, she felt more uneasy and more guilty than before.

She felt that this trip would not bring happiness, but that she would become more miserable as time passed.

23

When they boarded the plane for Rome, Ray was again seated beside Faith. They had been together constantly now for a week and she knew that it was no accident. She didn't know how Ray managed this, but what she did not know was that Ethel suspected what was happening and had decided not to interfere. It was not until later that Faith realized what was happening, but there was nothing that she could do about it. She couldn't be rude, so she continued to enjoy his friendship and his interesting conversation, hoping that she was mistaken in what she suspected.

As they neared the airport in Rome, Ray remarked, "We'll be going into Rome over the Appian Way, the way the Apostle Paul traveled when he was being taken to Rome as a prisoner. I'm sure, though, that you're familiar with the Bible account of that journey."

"I'm afraid not," she confessed. "I've just begun to read my Bible lately and I'm not too familiar with it yet."

"You'll never know all that's in it if you read it a lifetime," he stated. "I've been reading it ever since my teens when I was saved and I still wish I knew it better. I'm just thankful that I know it as well as I do, for it will make this part of the tour so much more interesting. You must not have been saved very long, or perhaps you've just neglected your Bible as so many Christians do."

"I wasn't too interested in it at first," she evaded, feeling like a hypocrite as she deceived him.

The burden of her deception and the terrible thing she had done weighed heavily upon her just then. How she wished she could tell him the truth and ask him what she could do to atone for that terrible thing when she had played with God and had made a mockery at that altar when she had so deceived Keith. But she didn't have the courage to tell him the terrible truth. He respected her now, but if she confessed, he would despise her and she wanted his respect. She would have to go on, growing more miserable under the conviction of this that was becoming more frightening every passing day. Though she still refused to believe that Jesus of Nazareth was the Son of God, or to accept Him as the Lord and Master of her life, she became more perturbed over her unbelief as time passed.

"This trip will grow more interesting in the light of the Bible," Ray remarked, "for we shall see so many evidences of fulfilled prophecy."

"That will be interesting," she replied, but she wondered if it really would.

On their way to the Mamertine prison, he was again beside her in the bus. She gave Ethel a reproachful glance as Ethel sat opposite with one of the girls, but Ethel gave her a knowing smile.

"I've been so anxious to see this place," Ray told her. "I've pictured Paul there so many times and wished that I could be where he was. Now the Lord has given me this opportunity."

When they went down the steps into the cold, damp cavern cut out of the solid rock, they understood why, perhaps, there had been no pictures of the place. Before them as they entered the dimly lighted room, there was an altar with candles burning and a crucifix and statues arranged upon the top of the altar.

"What a pity!" Ray murmured. "It destroys the sacredness of the place. If it had only been empty!"

During the guide's well-rehearsed and lengthy talk, Ray spoke in low tones to Faith as they stood apart from the rest.

"It was in this dreadful place that Paul wrote some of his most precious epistles. That last one he wrote to Timothy nearly always brings tears to my eyes as I read it. Are you familiar with it?" he asked. "I don't want to bore you if you are."

"No, please tell me," she said, for she did want to know.

"He wrote, 'I am ready to be offered up. I know that the time of my departure is at hand. I have fought a good fight. I have finished my course. I have kept the faith.' It wasn't too long after that he was taken out and beheaded, according to tradition. I pray that when the time of my departure comes, if the Lord tarries, I can say those same words, that I have kept the faith."

When they were once more in the bus, he said, "Paul made a statement that every Christian should rejoice over."

"What was that?" she asked, but she wasn't too much concerned about what Paul said. There was no cause of rejoicing within her nor could there be, whatever Paul might have said. Unbelief bore like a great weight upon her.

"He said, 'Henceforth there is laid up for me a crown of rejoicing, or rather a crown of righteousness, which the Lord, the Righteous Judge, shall give me in that day and not to me only, but unto all them also who love His appearing." He gave her a smile. "That's the easiest crown of all for a Christian to win when the Lord comes and when we stand before the judgment seat of Christ."

"I'm afraid I don't understand," she unwillingly admitted. She hated to display her ignorance, but she was curious and wanted to understand what he meant.

"It's easy because you don't have to do a thing, but just love the thought of His return. Just look for Him and hope for

His coming and try to live as if He were coming at any moment. Some Christians don't even seem to want Him to come, judging by the way they live."

"I'm afraid I've never learned much about that," she confessed.

"You must have been attending a church where His return is never mentioned."

"Perhaps I have," she agreed.

"The return of the Lord Jesus is the one great hope that keeps the Christian faithful and able to endure trials and even death," he told her. "Jesus told His disciples before He was crucified, that He would come again and that is the theme in many of Paul's epistles. I'll be glad to tell you more about it sometime," he offered.

She assured him that she would be interested, but she wondered if she really cared to hear any more.

When they visited the Catacombs, while the guide was giving his lecture, she was thinking of the people who had lived in these dark, cold caverns, who had suffered much because of their belief in a risen Christ. She wondered at the faith of these people in a Person who was only a man, though perhaps a great teacher, but no Messiah, and who surely was not able to rise from the dead as He declared that He would. The Lord Jehovah would never let His Son meet such a humiliating and terrible death. The Messiah would surely come in glory and the world would know when He came, she felt. He wouldn't die like Jesus of Nazareth died, like a criminal, nor would He live like a beggar. How could they believe such a thing? Yet there was Keith and here was Ray, each well-educated, and they believed. And all these other well-educated members of the party also believed. And this man called Paul the apostle, who wrote so many letters in the Christian Bible, had faith enough to die for it. It was all very confusing and disturbing. She had believed in the Lord God Jehovah until she had rebelled against that belief in her sorrow. She had mocked Him. What would her penalty be, she wondered.

When they were on their flight to Egypt, Ray was again

beside her and he began to talk of the place they were about to see.

"Egypt was once one of the great world powers," he commented, "but I'm sure you know that from history."

"I know that it was here that the Israelites were kept in slavery for hundreds of years," she replied.

"Yes, and after God had delivered them, later on God's prophets pronounced the doom of Egypt. One of them warned that Egypt would be nothing but a minor power and that surely has been fulfilled. Soon we'll be seeing other prophecy fulfilled. We'll be in the land where Moses grew up as a prince, but even though he would have been the heir to the throne, he gave it all up to be identified with his people. He knew that God had called him to lead His people out of slavery. God manifested His power in a wonderful way when he pronounced His judgments upon all the false gods of Egypt. Every plague was given to destroy faith in the power of those false gods. Have you read that part of your Bible?" he asked.

"Not yet," she admitted.

It was beginning to get dark and the waters underneath them became a black expanse.

He turned to her and asked, while his eyes rested upon the ring on her left hand, "Does that ring mean what I'm afraid it does?"

She held up her hand and looked at the ring while her eyes were shadowed with sorrow.

"It doesn't, any longer," she told him. "He was killed in a plane crash."

"Then may I ask you a question?" His eyes told her before he spoke, what she thought he was going to ask and she was sorry.

She had seen that expression in other eyes before and she knew the signs. She had seen it in Keith's eyes. The memory brought a stab of pain, but she tried to brush it aside. She must, if she wanted to carry on, and she knew she had to.

"Of course you may," she conceded, though she wished that he wouldn't ask it.

"If there is no one else, is there any hope for me? You must know that I care, even though we've known each other such a short time. Is there hope that you can care for me?"

She shook her head, while she gave him a tiny smile.

"I'm sorry to have to say no," she replied. "I like you so much and I admire you and respect you as a friend, but I'm afraid I can't give you hope for more."

"You don't mind if I still keep on hoping, because that's just what I'm going to do," he declared with a winsome smile.

"Please don't do that," she begged. "You will only be hurt and I don't want to hurt you."

"I've already been hurt, I've been stabbed in the heart," he said jestingly. Then more seriously, "I can't give up hope until I'm sure there is none for me. You see, I love you and when love comes, it dies slowly, if it ever dies. I should have known better when I first saw that ring, and I should have kept away from you, but I couldn't. You drew me like a flame draws a moth. I'm getting quite poetic, am I not?"

He tried to be jovial, but she saw he was trying to cover up his pain and disappointment. "I tried not to care," he added more seriously, "but love is something that comes even when we strive against it. It doesn't stop to ask questions and when it's there, there it is and there's nothing we can do about it. Will you let me keep on hoping? As I said, that's what I shall keep on doing."

She gave him a smile in answer to the brave one he gave her.

"I can't keep you from hoping, but I do want you to believe that I can't give you any hope. It seems that when — he died, all my love and the capacity for love died with him. I don't think that I have the capacity to love again."

"Promise me that if you feel that you can ever love someone again, you'll give me a chance," he begged.

"I promise," she agreed, "but I don't think I'll ever have to keep that promise."

"We shall see," he said and turned to look out the window.

"Look, there's old Egypt ahead of us," he said and he leaned over so that they could both look out together.

Cairo gleamed with a thousand lights and she was surprised to see how large it was. She was glad that he had changed the subject and she tried to banish thoughts that bore down upon her and made her unhappy and afraid. She wanted to enjoy her visit to this ancient city of the Pharaohs.

24

After a morning drive through the city of Cairo, the party had the thrill of sailing on the river Nile. Ethel sat on one side of Faith, while Ray sat on the other side.

"We didn't expect to have this trip," Ethel remarked. "It's a surprise. It's unbelievable that I'm actually here."

Her eyes were shining and some of her enthusiasm was shared by Faith and Ray.

"This boat isn't as gorgeous as Cleopatra's barge," Ray remarked, "but I'm sure that we're enjoying the ride as much as she did."

The next day they rode down beside the Nile and the guide pointed to the spot where Moses was supposed to have been found. Ethel smiled as she heard, for she had her doubts about the authenticity of the spot. She had learned to sift truth from error and tradition, but she did observe one thing and she remarked about it.

"We're seeing prophecy fulfilled here," she told Faith who was sitting by her. Ray was sitting opposite them.

"You mean about the flags?" he asked.

"Yes," she replied, then turned to Faith and explained, for she knew that Faith knew little about her Bible. "When

Moses was found somewhere near here, high flags were growing thick along the bank of the river. Otherwise Moses couldn't have been hidden and Pharaoh's daughter wouldn't have been coming here to bathe, for she would have been seen by people passing along the road. But see, there isn't the sign of even a blade of a flag anywhere. There is a prophecy in Jeremiah that predicts that the flags shall be dried up along the river and fishermen will no longer be spreading their nets."

"Perhaps that's because of the modern highways that have been built along and because of the building up of this section," Faith offered.

"That doesn't alter the truth of the prophecy," Ethel maintained. "It just proves over again that God knows the end from the beginning and that people should heed His warnings as well as believe His promises."

"That's quite a sermon, lady," Ray remarked. "I couldn't do better myself."

"Thanks, Reverend," she replied with a laugh. "Any time you need any further help, just call on me."

When they reached the Dead Sea, Faith was surprised to see how lovely it was. It was much larger than she anticipated, for her knowledge of Biblical geography was quite hazy. The waters were blue-green and waves lapped gently against the beach in front of the lovely modern hotel. The sea nestled in the spot below sea level between high mountains on either side. There was no sign of life on the beautiful expanse of waters, except the bathers near the shore. No seagulls floated gracefully over the waters searching for food, for there was no living thing in the waters.

"I never expected anything as beautiful as this," Ethel remarked.

They had unpacked the few necessary things and were sitting on the little balcony in front of their room watching the bathers.

"Over there on our right are the mountains of Moab. That land is where Naomi and her sons lived after her hus-

148

band died, while there was still a famine in Canaan. Do you remember?''

"You know I don't," Faith told her. "You know that I know so little about the Bible, for I haven't been reading it very long. Tell me about Naomi."

"To make it brief, her two sons married two Moabite women and both sons died afterward. When Naomi decided to return to her homeland, she told her two daughters-in-law to return to their people. Orpah went back, but Ruth wouldn't leave Naomi. She uttered those beautiful words that have been used in so many lovely songs: 'Entreat me not to leave thee. Whither thou goest, I will go; where thou lodgest I will lodge. Thy people shall be my people and thy God my God. Where thou diest I will die and there will I be buried.' Ruth later married Boaz and became the ancestress of David and through him of the Lord Jesus."

"That's a beautiful story," Faith commented.

Once more thoughts she had tried to bury, rose again to mar the joy, for the time being, of this part of the trip.

The next morning they rode toward Jerusalem. On the way the guide pointed out various spots of interest, places which Ethel knew to be authentic. They saw in the distance the blue-gray summit of Mt. Nebo and Ethel remarked to Faith that that was where Moses died.

"It seems such a pity that he was not allowed to enter the Promised Land," Ethel said.

"Why wasn't he?" Faith asked, again showing her ignorance of the Scriptures of her people.

"Because he disobeyed God just once," Ethel explained, realizing how little Faith knew of her Bible. She was glad that she could answer all of her questions thus far. "You see, once when there was no water, God told Moses to strike the rock and when he did, water poured out in a great stream. That rock represented Christ, who was smitten for our sins. When He was smitten for us, there came forth the living stream that brings eternal life to us and quenches our spiritual thirst. Then later on, when again there was no water, God told Moses to speak to the rock. But Moses was so angry with the people for their continual grumbling that he struck the rock in anger. God brought water, but Moses had to reap the penalty for that sin."

"That doesn't seem fair," Faith argued. "He shouldn't have been punished for that one little sin when he had been so faithful all along."

"But it wasn't a little sin," Ethel told her, "and with God, sin is sin, whether little or big. This was a big sin, for Moses not only disobeyed God, he destroyed the type, for Christ was only smitten once for all time. And God had to be just. When we disobey Him, He forgives, but we have to bear the consequences of our sin."

"How do you know that He forgave Moses?" Faith asked, still not believing in God's justice.

"Because He took Moses to the top of that mountain and showed him all of the land He had promised them, how beautiful it was and how it all belonged to his people. But he couldn't be allowed to go in, for then God wouldn't have been just. He would have condoned Moses' sin."

Faith was silent. She marveled at Ethel's knowledge of the Bible and she wished that she could have a faith like that, but she knew that it could never be.

They passed the ruins of Jericho and Ethel told her at her request, how Zaccheus had climbed into the tree in order to see Jesus as He passed and how salvation had come to him.

The nearer they came to Jerusalem, the more disturbed Faith became. She knew that from now on, everything she would see would be centered around the man Jesus. As they approached the city, she noticed how desolate much of the land was. There were rocks and large stones everywhere and there was so little land under cultivation. There were not many trees in the open country and she remarked about it to Ethel.

"The land looks so barren. I'm surprised. It surely doesn't look like a land flowing with milk and honey like you said it was when the spies brought back their report about it."

"That's another bit of prophecy being fulfilled that we're seeing," Ethel told her. "There's a place in the Bible that says that when people shall come from a far land and shall see the desolation, they shall ask, 'Why is the land like this?' And the answer shall come, 'Because they have forgotten God.' I believe, from what I've read, that we shall see quite a difference when we get to the kingdom of Israel.''

Finally they came to a stop when their passports were to be examined. Then they entered the City of David, where God promised that David's throne should be established forever.

"It makes me sad to know that all of this land is taken over by the Arabs," Ethel remarked. "Many of the most sacred places are in heathen hands. But then, that also is a fulfillment of prophecy. God's Word says that they shall seek to divide the land and they have already done that, but it will one day belong to the ones to whom God gave it. He told Abraham that his descendants should inhabit it forever and they shall own all of it some day.''

Faith was silent. She was trying to remember some of the things she wanted to tell her mother when she returned home. But how could she tell her some of the things she would like to tell her, when so much of it was centered about Jesus of Nazareth?

They reached their hotel, modern and beautiful, in the late afternoon, and after an enjoyable meal they sat in the lobby for a while.

"I'm glad that we can at last drink water," Ethel said. "I'm so tired of drinking bottled water."

During their tour through the Middle East, they were warned not to drink any water that had not been boiled, due to unsanitary conditions. Faith remembered that when they were lunching beside a stream near Beirut, she had seen a man bathing beside a water buffalo and a small boy was dipping up water and drinking nearby. She wasn't able to drink coffee after that, even if the water had been boiled.

As they walked up the steps leading to the Temple site, Ethel was humming the words of that beautiful song, "I walked today where Jesus walked."

"I heard that on the radio just before I left home," she

told Faith. "It was so appropriate in view of my trip that I couldn't help but shed a few tears. Just think, we're treading the path where the Lord Jesus trod and we'll be standing on the site where the Temple stood, where He drove the money-changers from the outer court. We'll stand upon the spot where the little children came to Him and worshiped Him in the Temple, when the Pharisees sought to rebuke them."

From there they drove to the Garden of Gethsemane. The group walked silently through the garden, beautiful in its restoration, as they remembered that it was there where their Saviour had sweat great drops of blood as He fought the battle against becoming that vile thing which bore the sin of the world — and in consequence of this, He would be separated from His Father who could not even look upon sin. The sinbearer He would become in His sinless person would in that moment for the first time be separated from his Father.

"I'm thinking of that beautiful poem," Ethel remarked as they emerged from the sacred quiet of the garden. " 'Into the woods my Master went and He was clean forspent.' Then it goes on to say, 'But the little gray leaves were kind to Him and the thorn tree had a mind to Him as into the woods He went.' And then it ends, 'It was on a tree they nailed Him last when out of the woods He came.' "

"How you love that Person!" Faith exclaimed. If she could only believe! But she knew she never could.

"He's not just a Person," Ethel corrected her. "He's my Saviour and soon-coming King."

Her eyes were moist, but they were aglow and Faith realized that Ethel had something that was priceless, something that she could never understand nor possess. How could her mother's religion ever bring such peace and assurance? The Lord Jehovah of her people seemed so far away. How could He ever bring this warmth and glowing faith that this girl had? This Jesus Ethel believed in seemed to be so very near, as if He was a living presence at her side and in her heart. It was wonderful, but how could they have such faith in someone who was just a man? It seemed so impossible and it was so confusing and she was becoming more confused and so much more heavily burdened.

She would be glad when they left this land and could go on to different sights. Perhaps then she would have more peace within her own soul. She was sorry she had come, much as she had enjoyed visiting the other places and much as she enjoyed Ethel and Ray, but she was angry with her father for playing this trick upon her about this trip. She didn't sleep well that night, but Ethel slept soundly and wakened refreshed and eager for the highlight of the whole trip, the visit to Gordon's Calvary and the Tomb.

Faith wished that she could skip this part of the tour, for she knew that there would be further disturbing emotions as she visited the place where a man had died a criminal's death, yet had changed the whole course of history. She still wondered how it could be. Try as she would, she could not find the answer and she didn't want to think about it. She wanted to get away from it all. She had come on this trip to see if she couldn't find more peace and less despair in her heart, but there was no peace, just disturbing emotions, questions, doubts, and the longing for something out of her reach.

25

On Sunday morning the party left soon after breakfast for the Tomb and Calvary. It was one of the authentic places in that land. Even as they were on their way, everyone seemed unusually silent. On their other bus trips, there had been laughter, joking and singing, but on this morning there was none of this. If anyone spoke it was in low tones. Faith thought that they acted as if they were actually going to a funeral of someone who had just died.

How silly it was for them to be so awed at the prospect of seeing the tomb of a man who was not what He claimed to be! But she had to admit that their faith was sincere and that their peace was real. She felt her own lack of peace now more than ever.

As these Christians approached the place where their Lord was buried and from which they believed He had risen, their hearts were filled with triumphant faith that would carry them through the rest of their lives.

When she thought of God as they neared the tomb, her fear grew greater. The memory of how she had lied when she went down to that altar and had pretended something that had not happened to her, overwhelmed her with the knowledge of her sin. What would her punishment be? She kept asking herself this question for which she knew no answer.

It was a perfect day. The sky was an unclouded azure canopy. As they drew up at the foot of the hill below the tomb and climbed to the top, the sun beamed warmly down upon them, though there was a cool breeze blowing that tempered the heat.

They entered the small enclosure that had been the garden of Joseph of Arimathea. It had been restored and was perhaps not as large as it had been originally, but it was lovely and immaculate. Not so much as a scrap of paper marred its beauty and orderliness. Flowers grew along the path that led to the tomb cut into the solid rock, and trees shaded the space between the beds.

The group entered silently. There was not so much as a whisper among them, for their hearts were filled with emotions that this sacred place with its memories stirred within them.

There were no other tourists there with their loud chatter and their ill-mannered pushing. Elsewhere they had had this experience, but it was not so here. Everything was silent. Even the birds had stopped their twittering as the group entered. The guide was introduced and he led the way down the few steps to the inside of the tomb. He stopped for a moment to show them the notches carved on either side of the entrance and remarked that this was probably the way the stone was closed or opened when it was placed over the entrance.

The chamber itself was small, just large enough to hold the group without crowding. And the tomb was empty. No altars, no candles, no statues or crucifix.

The guard explained as he showed them the opening at their left, that this was indeed a new tomb, as the Bible had stated, for this opening was what had been intended for another room that would hold another body. The excavation had never been finished.

He then indicated the narrow ledge that had been carved from the rocky wall in front of them and said, "Here is the place where our blessed Lord was laid." He indicated the raised place at one end where the head would rest.

As he continued his brief talk and gave it so reverently, emotion filled the hearts of those who stood there. Faith saw tears in the eyes of the women who stood near her.

Strange emotions began to filter through her own bitterness and unbelief. Here was the place where the body of Jesus of Nazareth had actually been placed. She could reach out and almost touch the place where the body of this Man who claimed to be the Son of God had been for at least three days. This Man who had laid down His life in the cruelest death known, who had done it willingly, for He could have escaped. She had read, as she scanned her Bible, so that Ethel would not suspect the truth, that He had told His disciples that He would be killed in Jerusalem when they were on their way there and she had read with a little feeling of satisfaction that neither did they believe nor understand. She didn't believe because she couldn't understand how His death could atone for the sin of the whole world. How could it be?

Yet as she stood there and listened to this Christian Arab give his brief message in such terms of reverence, she knew that he had been an unbeliever just as she was now, yet she knew that even he believed in this Man from Galilee. A feeling which she couldn't understand began to steal over her. It took possession of her in a strange way. If, after all, these people were right, what about her mother's people? They were rejecting someone who might, after all, be what He said He was.

When they went outside, they sat upon benches that were placed before the entrance to the tomb and one of the group began to sing. All of the others joined in singing "In the Garden" and then "He Lives." As she listened to the words and as her eyes were raised to that hill on her right, with the two round openings in its side and the longer one a little below that gave it the appearance of a huge skull, she knew that she was looking upon the hill called in the Hebrew tongue, Golgotha, the place of a skull. It was there that this Man who called Himself the Son of God endured such agony upon the cross where He was supposed to have shed His blood for the sins of everyone who believed.

One of the preachers took his place before the group and after a short prayer, began a brief message. He spoke of the cross and what it meant to the ones who believed, to those who went away from that cross to a new life of faith and peace. He mentioned that it was because Jesus Christ left the ivory palaces of heaven and came down to live as a man and to offer His life for their sin, that they could be sitting there today in this sacred spot thanking Him for the salvation that He brought, that everyone could receive by just believing. He mentioned what a privilege it was for them to be here on this morning, to be able actually to be in the place where the Lord gave His life for them and to know that someday He would return for those who had been faithful and who had believed.

As Faith listened, her eyes were fixed, not on the speaker, but on that rugged hill of Golgotha. A warmth began to seep into her innermost being. At first she was mystified, then she wondered, then became afraid. Suddenly, without any warning, a voice whispered within her, "It is true! He is the Son of God and He is alive today, for He rose from that very tomb that is now so empty."

She was startled, but suddenly she knew that what the voice said was true. It was true! He was the Son of God! His blood had been shed for her! And she was a lost sinner, a lost soul.

Suddenly she buried her face in her hands and began to sob audibly. As the minister finished his message and the group waited a moment before leaving, they heard her moan over and over again, "I do believe! I do believe! Oh, what is to become of me! God help me! God help me!"

Ethel put an arm around her and the tour director motioned the group to wait a moment. He realized that something wonderful had happened and he didn't want to interfere in any way.

"Tell me about it, dear," Ethel whispered as she held her. "Let me help you if I can."

"I believe! I believe!" Faith cried over and over. "What can I do? What can I do so that God will forgive me? I never really believed before. What can I do? What can I do?"

"You've done all that is necessary," Ethel assured her consolingly. "You have believed. Let's pray together and you can ask the Lord in your own words to forgive you and to give you the faith to believe that when you ask, He has forgiven you as He has promised in His Word."

"But you don't know!" Faith cried, still sobbing. "You don't know how terrible I've been when I pretended to believe and I didn't really."

"God understands and He knows," Ethel insisted. "I know He does, for He knows that you're sorry for everything that was displeasing to Him. Do you want me to pray for you?"

"Yes, please do," Faith sobbed.

Ethel prayed that Faith would understand and believe just what salvation means and that she would be willing to believe that the moment she asked God to forgive her sin of unbelief, that He would forgive her. Then she asked Faith to pray herself.

"You have to do the asking, my dear," Ethel told her. "Just ask God for yourself. I've done all that I can."

"But I've never prayed," Faith confessed. "All the time I knelt there when you prayed, I wasn't praying. I was just pretending, so that you wouldn't discover the truth. I'm afraid that God can't forgive that sin. It was so terrible."

"Jesus said that 'he that cometh to me I will in no wise cast out.' That means you. All you have to do is to say that you know you've done wrong and ask God to forgive you for Jesus' sake."

Faith repeated the words, and then in an agony of confession she poured out such a prayer of contrition that those who heard it listened with tears.

When she finally rose to her feet, her face was radiant, though it was drenched with tears. The sun shone upon her through the trees and Ray thought she had never looked so beautiful.

"Will you stay just a little longer?" she asked as the group rose to leave. "I want to confess to you what God already knows and for which I've asked His forgiveness. I thank Him that I believe He has forgiven me and I'm so glad that it was in this holy place that I received His forgiveness and His pardon and salvation."

They sat down and waited for her to speak.

"It's a long story, but I'll make it as short as possible," she began. "I am part Jewish. My mother is Jewish. When she married, the marriage caused such sorrow in the lives of her parents and my father's, that it has followed them all of their lives, even though they loved each other very much. When I was born, they agreed not to try to press me for belief in either my mother's faith or my father's, until I was old enough to decide for myself. Consequently I grew up with nothing and when I did try to accept either one or the other's faith, they had nothing to give me and I believed nothing. My mother had tried to indoctrinate me in her belief, but all she succeeded in doing, was to make me believe that Jesus was not the Son of God and not our Messiah.

"After I became engaged, the boy I was to marry accepted Christ as his Saviour and I learned that he couldn't marry me unless I believed like he did. I loved him enough to want to do what he wanted me to do, so I made a pretense of believing, though I never believed at all. He was killed in an airplane accident. After that I became bitter against God and I sometimes doubted that I even believed in Him. Now at last I do believe and how I thank Him for leading me here so that I could believe and be saved."

For a moment there was silence while some wiped their eyes, then they rose to leave. As she turned to leave with Ethel, the guide at the tomb came and shook hands with her.

"I'm glad you believe," he said. "I was once like you. I too thought Jesus was a myth and an imposter. Now I believe, just as you do."

"What you said there in the tomb had much to do with it," she told him. "I knew that you were an Arab, and that you had had the same doubts that I had. If you could believe in Jesus as the Son of God, why should I continue to doubt? It all came over me there in the tomb while you were talking.''

His eyes became moist and his voice trembled as he told her how glad he was to hear that, that he had helped someone to find Christ.

When they were seated in the bus, Faith found herself again beside Ray. She was sorry, because she wanted to talk to Ethel.

''That was a brave thing you did back there,'' he said. ''I can't tell you how glad I am that you found peace at last. I knew how bitter you were in your sorrow. I've been praying that you would find the peace that only God can give through Christ.''

She looked at him in surprise.

''You were praying for me!'' she gasped. ''How I do thank you! Perhaps your prayers made possible what happened.''

''I hope that they had a little part, at least,'' he told her.

She was nearer to loving him then than she had ever thought she could be. If he had done any praying at all, she thought it would have been that she would love him and not for her soul.

That night when she knelt beside Ethel, she said, ''Tonight I shall really be praying and not pretending. How can God forgive such sin! I'll have a lot of praying to get caught up with.''

For the first time in all of her life, she lay down to sleep with absolute peace in her heart. For the first time she went to sleep with a whispered prayer upon her lips, a prayer of thanksgiving. There was no bitterness in her heart when she thought of Keith. And how she thanked her father for the trick he had played upon her! What would her life have been if she had not come! How glad he would be when he knew that his little scheme and his prayer for her had worked the miracle for which he hoped.

26

Faith was surprised and overcome to the point of tears by the reaction of the group after she had made her confession. Instead of avoiding her as she had expected them to, each one of them came to her during the rest of the day and told her how glad they were about what the Lord had done for her.

That night as they were returning from a service in a little mission church where Faith had witnessed for the first time what true worship was, she sat next to Ray. She had been very interested when she saw the little group of Christians there — people who had been converted from the religion of Mohammed. They had undoubtedly been just as stubborn as she had been. She was surprised to see such a number of old men in the group. Though she couldn't understand the language of the sermon, the young minister was putting his whole soul into his message and she saw the rapt attention that his audience paid to his words. She could enter into the spirit of the meeting even if she couldn't understand the words.

"I noticed that you enjoyed the service, even though we couldn't understand the words," Ray remarked as they drove along. "It was your first experience in a Christian service since you've become a believer. I'm sure you'll never forget it.''

"No, I never could forget it,'' she agreed. "It was wonderful. For the first time I could feel the presence of God there.''

"Now I know why I couldn't hope that you could care for me,'' he said, "Even though I told you that I'd keep on hoping. It was of the Lord. It would have been a tragedy, if you had said yes and still not been a believer.''

"I know that,'' she admitted. "I was made aware of that not long ago when I did that terrible thing and lied to the man I loved and played with God about such a serious thing. It's so wonderful to know that the Lord forgave me and saved my poor unworthy soul.''

"Now that you are a real born-again believer, may I really hope that you can learn to care?''

His voice was appealing and her heart was stirred as it had never been by Mark. But she remembered how she had hurt Mark so terribly and she didn't want to make another serious mistake.

"I'll be honest with you,'' she told him. "I like you very much and I was very near to loving you this afternoon, but I don't want you to hope, for I'm afraid that if you do you'll be hurt. In the beginning, after — he — died, I did a terrible thing to another boy who wanted to marry me. I was so hopeless and lonely that I thought if I could make him happy, I'd marry him. I thought that perhaps I could learn to care for him, even though my heart seemed so dead and unable to love again. Then, so near the time of the wedding, I just couldn't go through with it and he was hurt and angry — and he had a right to be. I don't want anything like that ever to happen again.''

"But now it's different,'' he argued. "You have the love of God in your heart and you have the capacity for love. And you'd make a wonderful preacher's wife,'' he added with a smile.

"I doubt that, for I'm still ignorant of the Bible and such a feeble young Christian.''

"I'm willing to take a chance on that," he asserted. "Just promise that you'll try to care. I wouldn't want you to marry me if you didn't."

"Please give me time," she begged. "I know that love is something that comes without being coaxed, without a person having to try to bring it to life. Just now I'm too confused about many things. I'm happy and yet I still grieve. These two emotions are not easy to cope with."

"I'll help you, if you'll let me try," he persisted.

"I surely need all the help I can get," she said with a little laugh, "so you're welcome to try, but I'm not making any promises."

"I'll just keep on hoping — and praying," he told her.

She wondered if it would be possible for her to really love him. There was something about him, beside his attractive personality and good looks, that appealed to her. Was it because he was a Christian or was it because he was awakening something within her heart that she had thought gone forever with Keith's going? As she pondered this, she became confused, but she was happier in a different way than she had ever been. There was a peace within her, a peace which Keith had tried to make her believe, but which she had doubted as a reality. She knew that whatever she might face in the future, joy or sorrow, there would always be that abiding peace deep within her that she had not had.

Ray said nothing more about his love, but she could see it in his every glance, read its tones beneath his conversation. Though it disturbed her, it did not make her unhappy as it had done before.

When they entered the kingdom of Israel the next day, Faith could look with keener interest at what she saw in this land that belonged to her people according to God's promise to Abraham. A new thought came to her as they stopped at the Mandelbaun Gate to have their passports examined. She could no longer say that the Jews were her people, for now that she was a Christian, she was neither Jew nor Gentile, she was a child of God. She had heard that before when she had attended the church with Keith, but it had never made any impression upon her because she was not really listening. It was a wonderful thought. Perhaps some day her mother might be made to realize this same truth. She would pray that this would happen.

When they waited at the gate until they were given the order to pass, she was surprised to note that there was really no gate and she saw no barbed wire entanglements which she had expected to see and about which she had read. However, on either side of the border there were two-story houses and in the windows of these houses there were sandbags piled high, while in between the sandbags, the guard pointed out that there were guns which were trained on each side of the border. There were frequent disturbances along the border and Ray remarked that he wondered how long it would be before actual fighting began again.

As they traveled north, Faith saw a change in the surrounding scene. They passed through evergreen forests and along the road there were fertile fields. She saw olive groves, orchards, and citrus groves. Every foot of the land seemed to be under cultivation. It was so different from what she had seen in Jordan.

The guide told them that the Jews had spent millions in reforestration, for, during the war, almost all the trees had been destroyed.

"That's another prophecy fulfilled," Ethel whispered to Faith as they sat side by side.

The guide explained how these trees had been watered and he showed them the expensive system of irrigation that had been used for field and forest. Then he made a remark that brought a low exclamation from Ethel.

"This year there has been so much rain in the spring that no irrigation was needed."

"That is God's Word being proved true," Ethel told Faith. "He promised that in the latter days the former and the latter rains would be restored, just as He warned, long before, that they would be taken away, because of Israel's sin. How wonderful to see all this happening under our very eyes!"

This time Faith's enthusiasm and thrill were just as strong as Ethel's.

"It's wonderful," she agreed. "How I wish I knew my Bible as well as you know yours. I surely have a lot to learn."

"But you'll love every minute of it," Ethel assured her.

Faith knew that she would. No more pretense of reading something she was supposed to be reading and enjoying. Now she would really try to learn what she had so long neglected and she knew that she would not only enjoy it, but that she would be helped and strengthened in her newly-found faith.

They had the thrilling experience of riding on the Sea of Galilee, after having spent a night on its shores in a beautiful modern hotel. As they looked out over the dark waters under a starry sky before they prepared for bed, Ethel remarked, "Just think, we're here on the shores of the very lake where Jesus spoke to the storm and instantly the wind stopped and the sea became calm. No wonder those disciples asked, 'What manner of man is this, that even the wind and the waves obey Him?' "

"I'll be thinking about that tomorrow," Faith said. "And I'll be remembering that if the Lord hadn't saved me, I would have doubted the whole story and I would have thought how foolish all of you were to believe such a myth."

"I'm glad it happened in time for you to enjoy the rest of the trip," Ethel told her. "What a pity it couldn't have happened sooner."

"But I wouldn't have wanted it to happen in any other way or in any other place," Faith contradicted. "That scene will remain with me as long as I live."

As they rode on the lake of Galilee from Tiberius to the place where the modern town of Capernaum was, Ethel pointed out the mountains on the other side of the lake.

"Over there is the place where Jesus healed the demoniac. I always smile when I read that account. Those demons didn't want to be without a body, so they begged Jesus to let them enter the bodies of that herd of swine feeding near. Jesus knew what would happen and He gave them permission, but when they entered the swine, those hogs ran down the mountainside and were drowned. So the demons didn't have any bodies, after all.''

They visited ruins that might have been the only remaining vestige of what had been the city of Capernaum, a ruined pagan temple, then they rode toward Nazareth. When they reached the place where the village had been, the guide took them past the place where Jesus was supposed to have been dragged by the mob after He had proclaimed Himself to be their Messiah, when they intended to cast Him down over the side to a terrible death upon the rocks below.

''But they couldn't kill Him and He just passed through that mob,'' Ethel told Faith. ''They couldn't kill Him because His time had not yet come and God had planned that He should die on a cross, not at the hands of an unbelieving mob.''

Faith listened with an eager, open mind and heart, for she was learning from this dedicated young Christian how wonderful God and His Word were.

When they finally reached London on the last lap of their trip, Faith knew that she would soon be at home again and that she would be lonely after having been all this time with these friends whom she had grown to love. She wondered how her mother would react when she learned of her salvation. She knew that, in spite of loneliness and heartache, she would never be down in the depths of despair, for she now had One upon whom she could cast her burden and she knew that He would give her the strength she would need to go on and live the life He would have her live.

There was one problem she knew she would have to face before they reached New York. That was Ray and the question she knew he would ask. She had felt that she was being unkind as she maneuvered to sit beside Ethel when she knew that Ray wanted to sit with her, but she wanted time to think. The more she thought about it, the more convinced she was that she couldn't give him any encouragement. If this had happened before she had had the experience at Calvary, she might have encouraged him as she had done Mark, for she felt very near to loving him and she hated to think that when the trip was over, she might never see him again.

After they had returned from watching the changing of the guard at Buckingham palace, and they were alone for a little while in the lobby, Ray reproached her.

"You've been avoiding me," he told her. "Does that mean that I've had my answer? Was that a nice way to let me down?"

He tried to smile, but his eyes were serious and Faith knew that he was hurt.

"I wasn't letting you down," she denied. "But I did want more time to think."

"If it's taken you all this time to make up your mind, I'm afraid that the answer has already been decided."

"I just don't know what to say," she admitted. "Please give me a little more time."

"But we don't have much time left," he insisted. "After tomorrow we'll all be separated and we may never meet again."

"That's what worries me. I want to see you again and I thought that perhaps you might come to see me after I've been at home for a while and had had an opportunity to think things over and analyze my own feelings. But I wouldn't want to suggest that, if I wasn't sure that I might be able to love you. I just don't know what to say."

"If that's the way you feel, I'll cling to that little thread of hope," he told her and his smile was much brighter.

"I promise that I'll pray about it and tomorrow after we return from Stratford on Avon, I'll give you a definite answer. I don't want to say no," she added with a little smile.

Just then the others joined them for the trip to Westminster Abbey and the Houses of Parliament.

As Faith sat beside Ethel, she was so disturbed and so undecided about the situation that she didn't look forward to the trip with any degree of pleasure.

When she prayed about her problem that night, she was still undecided, for she had received no real leading from the Lord. She thought that perhaps she was too young in the experience in prayer to understand the leading of the Lord. When, however, she went down to breakfast the next morning, she knew that if she really loved Ray, there would be no question, no struggle to decide what to tell him. Her heart would have cried out to her to say yes. She knew that she must tell him that there was no hope for him. Perhaps she would never be able to love anyone again. But it would be better for her and for Ray, than for her to try something that she had tried with Mark and to have it end the same way.

She hated to tell Ray and she decided to put it off until the very last, so that the trip would not be spoiled.

27

Just after breakfast the group met in the lobby. They chattered and laughed while waiting for the bus to arrive. They were looking forward to an interesting trip through the English countryside on the way to the birthplace of Shakespeare and the cottage where Ann Hathaway had lived.

When she noticed how nervous and eager Ray appeared, Faith was almost persuaded to tell him that she would try to love him, for she dreaded the thought of never seeing him again. She knew that if there had never been a Keith in her life, she would have fallen in love with him before now. She gave Ray a smile and it seemed to encourage him, for his anxious expression vanished and a more cheerful and hopeful light shone from his eyes.

"This is a perfect morning," he remarked as he sat beside her. "As a superstitious person would say, 'I'll take that as a good omen.'"

"But you're not superstitious," she parried.

Just then the bus started and they began the drive through the city traffic. One of the boys had bought a copy of one of the New York papers which had a foreign edition for tourists. He glanced over the headlines as they drove through traffic.

Suddenly he turned to the girl sitting beside him and exclaimed, "Listen to this! Someone has been found still alive from that plane that was wrecked at sea a few months ago near North Vietnam. The article says that this flyer has a fantastic story to tell, but that he has been advised not to reveal it until government agencies have had time to check with him. He's in a hospital in California. He's so terribly emaciated that the hospital attendants don't see how he could still be alive. Boy! What an experience he must have had!"

"Does it say who he is?" the girl asked.

"Wait a minute," he said while he scanned the article. "Yes. His closest relative, his mother, has been notified. His name is Keith Loring."

He turned to Faith and said, "He's from your home town. Do you know him?"

Faith didn't answer him. At the mention of Keith's name, she uttered a little cry and the world seemed to spin around her madly as she lost consciousness for a moment and slumped down in the seat.

Ray caught her and held her in his arms while consciousness slowly returned. As she opened her eyes and looked into his white face, she knew that he knew. Now he had his answer. Even in that moment of whirling thoughts and returning consciousness, she felt sorry for him.

He held her a moment silently, while she regained her strength and her full composure. She released herself from his arms and looked into his stricken eyes while she tried to control herself.

"Is it true? Is it true?" she asked in a weak, trembling voice. "Did he really say that that flyer was Keith? Keith Loring?"

Ray nodded. He couldn't say a word.

"Please let me see that article," she asked of the boy in front of her.

"Sure," he said, handing her the paper and pointing to the article down in the corner of the front page. She read the article with wide eyes while Ray sat silent beside her. He knew that the end of his hopes had come. When Faith finished reading and had actually seen Keith's name in print, she handed the paper to the boy, then she covered her face with her hands and burst into tears.

"This is no time for crying," Ray told her. "You should be rejoicing and thanking God for a miracle."

"I'm so happy I just can't keep from crying," she sobbed. "It was a miracle. I shall never cease to thank God for it." She dried her eyes and tried to be more calm. "It just doesn't seem possible," she repeated over and over again. "To think that all the time when I was suffering so much and was so bitter toward God, Keith was still alive and God knew that He would bring him back to me. And to think of the terrible mistake I almost made back there at home."

Ray said nothing and she looked into his eyes and saw that he was suffering now even while she was so happy.

"I'm so sorry," she said. "I wish there was something that I could do or say, but I know there is nothing."

"No, there is nothing," he agreed. "But I know that I can bear it. If it should have been different, God would have arranged it that way."

There was silence for a moment, then he turned to her while his face was still white and his eyes were so full of sadness that it hurt her to look at him.

"What would the answer have been if this hadn't happened?" he asked.

"It would have been no," she said sadly. "I tried to think that I could tell you that I loved you or that I would try, but every time I thought of telling you that, the image of Keith seemed to stand in the way. I couldn't forget the love I still had for him. I'm so glad that God didn't let me make another mistake. You would have been hurt even more and I wouldn't want that to happen to you. I shall always remember you as the finest man I ever met."

"Next to Keith," he replied with a smile. "Don't let your happiness be spoiled by thinking of me. I've met disappointments before now and I'm sure that I can meet this without letting it get the best of me. Let's enjoy the day together and you be just as happy as you are bound to be."

"Thank you," she said. "I'm so grateful and you're so wonderful."

He turned away for a moment, for he didn't want her to see his weakness. Presently he turned back to her and began to comment upon the scenery as they passed along the lovely countryside.

When Faith had the opportunity to tell Ethel that Keith was still alive, Ethel rejoiced with her.

"I feel sorry for Ray," Ethel commented. "I know that he was in love with you almost from the beginning and I was hoping that you would fall in love with him, especially after what happened at Calvary."

"I tried to, but I couldn't," Faith told her. "Now I know that it was God who kept me from making a second mistake. Ray's such a wonderful person. Some girl will have a wonderful husband."

During the rest of the trip Ray sat with her and as they visited the different places of interest, he talked as cheerfully as if nothing had happened to destroy his hopes. She was grateful for this and she was glad that they could visit these interesting places without anything to mar the pleasure of the trip, as far as outward appearances were concerned.

Her one desire now was to return home as quickly as possible and then, if it were possible, to fly to the west coast and see Keith. She was glad that they were leaving the next morning for home.

When they had passed through customs in New York and were on their way to different hotels, Faith had a moment alone with Ray.

"It's been wonderful knowing you," she said while his eyes looked into hers as if he would stamp the image of her forever upon his heart. "May I kiss you good-by?" she asked as he held her hand in a farewell clasp.

"Of course. Why not?" he replied.

She drew nearer and he held her in his arms for a moment as their lips met for a brief instant, careless of who might be watching.

"I hope you won't forget me, because I'll never forget

you," she said as he held her for a moment longer.

"As if I ever could forget you!" he exclaimed in a voice that trembled in spite of himself.

He watched her as she went through the doors and to the waiting taxi. Deep within him there was pain, but there was also the prayer that the Lord would give him strength to bear that pain and to live so that he would be the stronger for having experienced it.

When Faith finally reached home, her parents were both at the airport to meet her. Her father was the first to speak after they had embraced and held each other for long moments.

"I've good news for you, honey," he said. "How good the Lord has been!"

"I know that good news already," she told him with a happy smile. She told him how she had heard the news. "Daddy, I want to go to Keith right away, if I can," she said. "Do you think they will let me see him?"

"I'm sure they will," he told her. "I'll see about it and make arrangements as soon as we get home."

"Thank you, Daddy," she said, leaning against him and sighing happily.

Her mother said little. She was trying to be happy over what had happened. She knew that she might as well get used to Keith as a son-in-law, for what her husband had said must be true. It was the will of God and who was she to try to rebel against that will?

"I've got something to tell you when we get home," Faith told her father.

During the ride home, while she talked about her trip, underneath all her chatter, her heart was singing a little song, "Keith is alive! Keith is alive! Oh thank You, Lord, for all of Your goodness to me when I've been so unworthy. Thank You, thank You, Lord!"

28

"Now what was that wonderful thing that you had to tell me?" Faith's father asked as soon as they reached home and she had put her luggage in her room and they were seated in the living room.

Faith hesitated a moment. She had wanted to tell him the wonderful news when they were alone, but she knew that she would want to tell her mother also, so she thought perhaps it was best that she should tell it now.

"I believe it was the answer to your prayers when you chose this trip for me," she began. "When I first found out that the group was a group of Christians, I was angry with you, because I thought you had played a trick on me. If I could have left then, I would have done so, but I didn't find out until we were on our way."

Her father smiled, but said nothing, while her mother looked on silently, wondering what was coming.

"How glad I am that I couldn't turn back!" she exclaimed. "They were all so friendly and my roommate, Ethel, was such a lovely girl that I fell in love with her from the beginning.

"I know you were praying for me, Daddy, for you said

you would be," and she gave him a look that brought a glow to his heart. "I was so bitter and such a doubter that I thought all those people were misguided to believe the things they said they believed. Even when Ethel showed me so many evidences that the prophets in the Old Testament had foretold what we saw was actually happening, and so many of their prophecies had already been fulfilled, I didn't believe. God was speaking to me all the time. I know it now, though I didn't realize it then. It just made me unhappy and I was miserable, for I knew how I had deceived Keith. I had made him believe that I had accepted Christ as my Saviour when I still didn't believe that He was the Son of God. I began to realize what a wrong I had committed and I was afraid. But I refused to believe. When we went to the tomb that Sunday morning and I stood in the very place where Christ's body was laid and when I saw that grim hill where He was crucified and when I heard the reverent words from that Arab Christian who believed in Him, and while I was listening to the message that one of the preachers gave, I looked up at the hill of Calvary — and suddenly I knew, Daddy, for a voice spoke to my soul, that Jesus was the Son of God. I began to cry and to ask God to forgive me for being such a sinner. I was afraid they would despise me when they knew the truth about me, but they were so wonderful and so glad that I had found Jesus Christ as my Saviour. I've been so happy in the Lord ever since, even when I still thought that Keith was dead."

She turned to her mother who had sat silent and frozen.

"Mother, if you had been there, you would have believed, too. I wish that I could make you understand just what happened to me. Everything I saw in the land of Palestine and everything that Ethel pointed out to me from the Bible, made me realize that God's Word had to be true, even when I still didn't want to believe. I'll be so happy to try to make you see what I've seen, so that you can be as happy as I am, for there is such hope for the Christian that our people can never know."

"I don't want to talk about it," her mother said in a dull voice. Presently she left the room.

Faith turned to her father.

"I know she will believe before long," she stated, "because both of us shall be praying for her. God will hear and answer our prayers."

Her father took her in his arms and held her close. His voice was far from steady as he spoke.

"I believe we shall win. I did pray for you, but I'm afraid I didn't have much faith. Our God is a great God. I'll try never to doubt again."

Faith went to sleep with a prayer of thanksgiving for herself and a prayer for her mother's salvation upon her lips.

The next evening when her father came home, he told her that he had made arrangements for her to leave for the west coast the next day and he had the assurance that she would be able to see Keith as soon as she got to the hospital.

It wasn't many hours before she was admitted to Keith's room. She was shocked when she saw him. He was still so emaciated that he looked like a living skeleton. His left arm was in a cast and there were bruises upon his face and upon his shoulders.

He smiled at her and held out his one thin arm as the nurse led her into the room.

"They told me you were coming and I've been counting the hours until now," he said in a voice that was still weak. "How I prayed over there that I would live to see you again."

She knelt by the bed and laid her cheek against his, while the nurse discreetly withdrew.

"How good the Lord was to spare you and give you back to me," she murmured. "I'll never be able to thank Him enough for this."

"The doctor says that I'll be as good as ever, but that it will take time. I won't be able to travel until this arm is out of the cast. It was neglected so long that they thought at first it would have to be amputated, but they managed to save it. I thank the Lord for that as well as everything else that happened."

"Tell me what happened," she said.

"I've been told not to say much about it and not to give out any information to any newsmen, for security reasons," he told her. "I think it has to do with my escape, for it involves soldiers who were in the secret loyal army and are working through the underground. When we were almost in sight of the land, our plane seemed to fall apart. When the first shock came, Roger who was sitting next to me, reached over and opened the escape hatch and pushed me out. Before he could follow me, while I was dropping down, the plane exploded and parts of the wreckage were flying all about me.

"I hit the water and my lifebelt saved me, for we were all equipped with them. Even so, I hit the water with such force that I went under for a few moments. I suppose the impact knocked me out for a while, for before I really knew what had happened to me, someone in a motorboat picked me up and took me to shore and to some building where they put me through the third degree with a vengeance. I never saw Roger again. He saved my life but lost his own by doing it. He was the best friend I ever had," he said.

"They beat me when I wouldn't answer their questions and then they put me in a stockade where I was not only exposed to the weather, but I was slowly being starved to death. They would come at intervals and ask me questions about our destination and other questions that I couldn't answer and which I wouldn't have if I could. We didn't know our destination, for we were flying under sealed orders known only to the chief officer and the pilot. And all of them were blown to bits," he added sorrowfully.

"I'm not allowed to tell even you the details about my escape until I have permission, but I can say this much. When I was so weak that I could scarcely walk, it was by the aid of a Christian national and this soldier who was connected with the Christian underground that I got away. My arm was broken not long before I escaped, when some brute struck me with his club because I didn't answer his questions. It wasn't attended to until I was on my way here."

He was out of breath and she realized how weak he still was.

Later she told him what had happened to her and she made a full confession of her deception.

"I did it because I wanted you more than I wanted God, or anything else," she said. "I began to realize on that trip what a terrible thing I had done. But the Lord has forgiven me and I want you to forgive me too."

"Since I never knew, there's nothing to forgive," he replied. "Now I want to know how soon you'll marry me."

"Whenever you want me to," she told him.

"Then let's make it right away," he said. "That is, if you're willing to take care of a semi-invalid for a while."

"That would be the greatest joy of my life," she assured him with a smile, leaning over to kiss him.

The nurse and the chaplain of the hospital made all the necessary arrangements and in a few days he came with two of the nurses and performed the ceremony. Faith smiled as she thought of the wedding dress which she had planned for this occasion. It was quite a contrast to the simple suit which she wore.

When they were alone at last, after a little party attended by the nurses on Keith's floor, the doctor and the chaplain, Keith asked, "What will your parents think when you wire them?"

"Dad will be delighted, and I think in time Mom will be happy too, for I'm sure that God will be able to change her."

"How strange and how wonderful are the ways of the Lord!" Keith remarked. "We have both gone through times of trial and suffering, but I know that it was all for a purpose and that we shall be stronger for having endured all that has happened to us."

"I'm thinking of a verse that Ethel used to quote to me when I didn't believe. Philippians 4:13, 'I can do all things through Christ who strengtheneth me.' Since He has led us along the way this far, I know that He will give us strength to go the rest of the way, no matter what happens to us."

"How right you are, Mrs. Loring," he said as he drew her to him and their lips met in a clinging, tender kiss.